CHUCK THE MONK

EMPTY FUN

Celo & Tyler

Catlike daily wisdom and
the quest for the feline Self

Title: Chuck the monk — Empty fun
www.chukthemonk.com
© Diego Fernando Otero Paredes
© Carlos Eduardo Valencia Alfonso
© The ZenLab
ISBN: 978-94-92662-01-9

To our cosmic Self

Foreword

Like any other entity, I am the outcome of interdependence. I was created in the minds, hearts, and hands of two friends who are having a lot of fun with my purrs.

I was always interested in who we are, consciousness, the mind, and how all that stuff works. So I ended up being a well-trained but poorly-skilled brain scientist. Along that pathway, I discovered Zazen and became a modern monk. By taking refuge in the three treasures and through a devoted practice, subjective realization and intuition started their own path in my life. This, of course, led to a variety of situations, thoughts, and feelings that are reflected in our strips. They mostly involve a dialectic relation between science and spirituality, the perks of being a lay monk, dealing with attachment, meditation retreats, living Buddhism in western cultures, work, morality and of course, a lot of love and compassion.

The guys and I feel very passionate about communicating and inspiring both thoughts and feelings to other sentient beings through this project. For us, it feels like a very organic process, not only because we put a lot of heart and guts in it, but also because it grew by itself, it came together and developed in a natural way. Currently, we are kind of discovering together with great curiosity and joy, where it will take us.

This book presents our first year of weekly online purrs. It has been a wonderful process with ups and downs, where we all played, experimented and learned with the impermanence of different toys, styles, and techniques that we hope you savor. Each purr is preceded by a meow. They are meant to be chewed both apart and, like everything else, interdependently. Chew them wisely, slowly, maybe not in your sandbox.

So here we are, showing you the result of our crossing paths. We certainly hope you enjoy it and that it has a tickling poke in your emotions and minds.

With all our kindness, gratitude and affection,

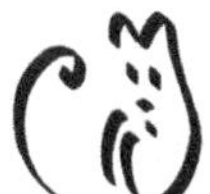

Chuck the monk*

*Also on behalf of Diego and Carlos, with whom I share this beautiful interdependent existence.

An identity thief found
nothing here to be stolen.
He didn't walk empty handed though,
as he carries with him a precious lesson.

Buddhist

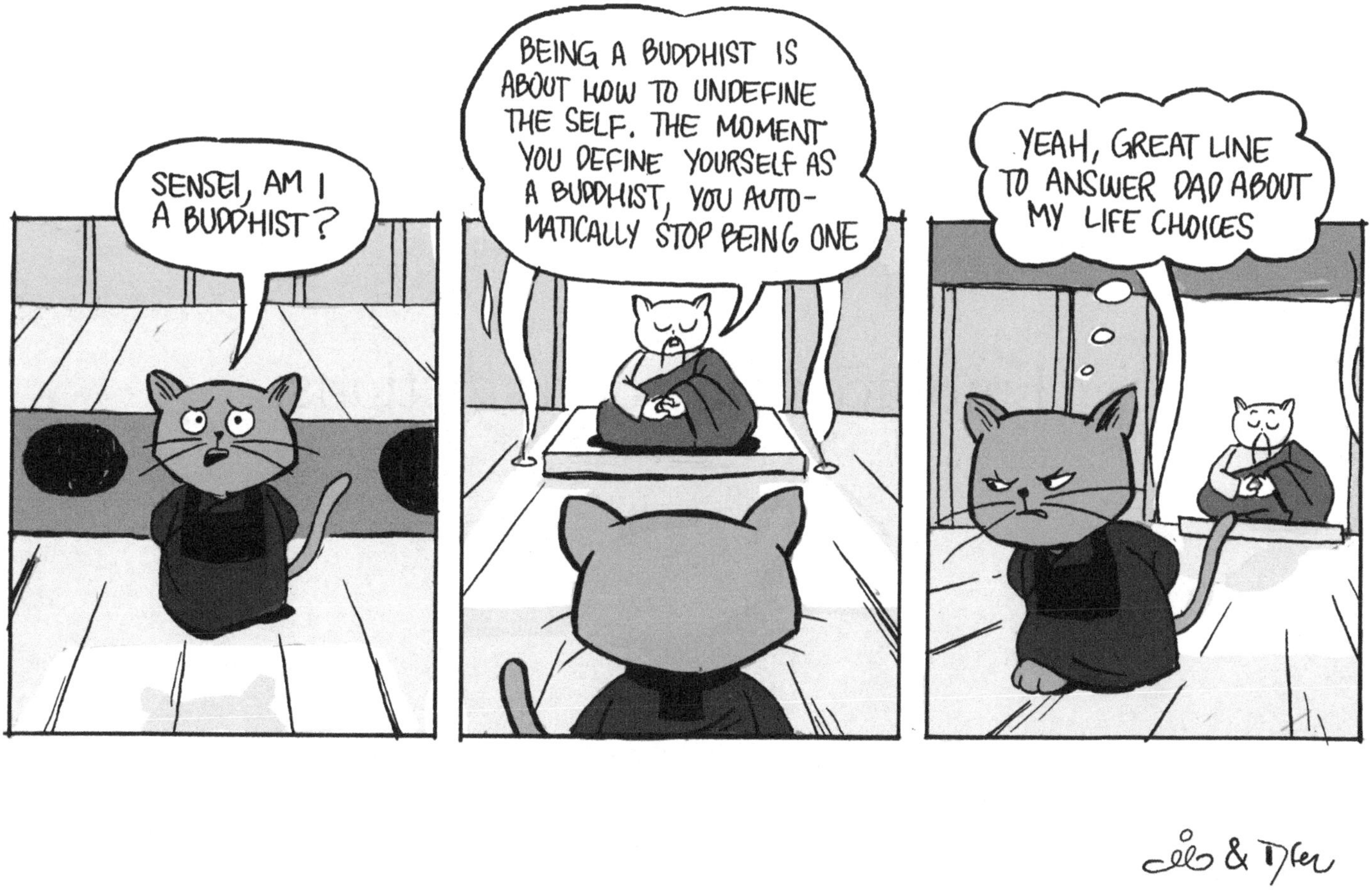

SENSEI, AM I A BUDDHIST?
BEING A BUDDHIST IS ABOUT HOW TO UNDEFINE THE SELF. THE MOMENT YOU DEFINE YOURSELF AS A BUDDHIST, YOU AUTO-MATICALLY STOP BEING ONE
YEAH, GREAT LINE TO ANSWER DAD ABOUT MY LIFE CHOICES

Embrace your contradictions.

Irony

AND THIS IS THE MONASTERY SHEEP. HER NAME IS IRONY
FUNNY NAME, WHY DO YOU CALL HER THAT?
SHE'S ALLERGIC TO WOOL
ATCHOO!

Apparently, flies have a lot of fun.

Thursday

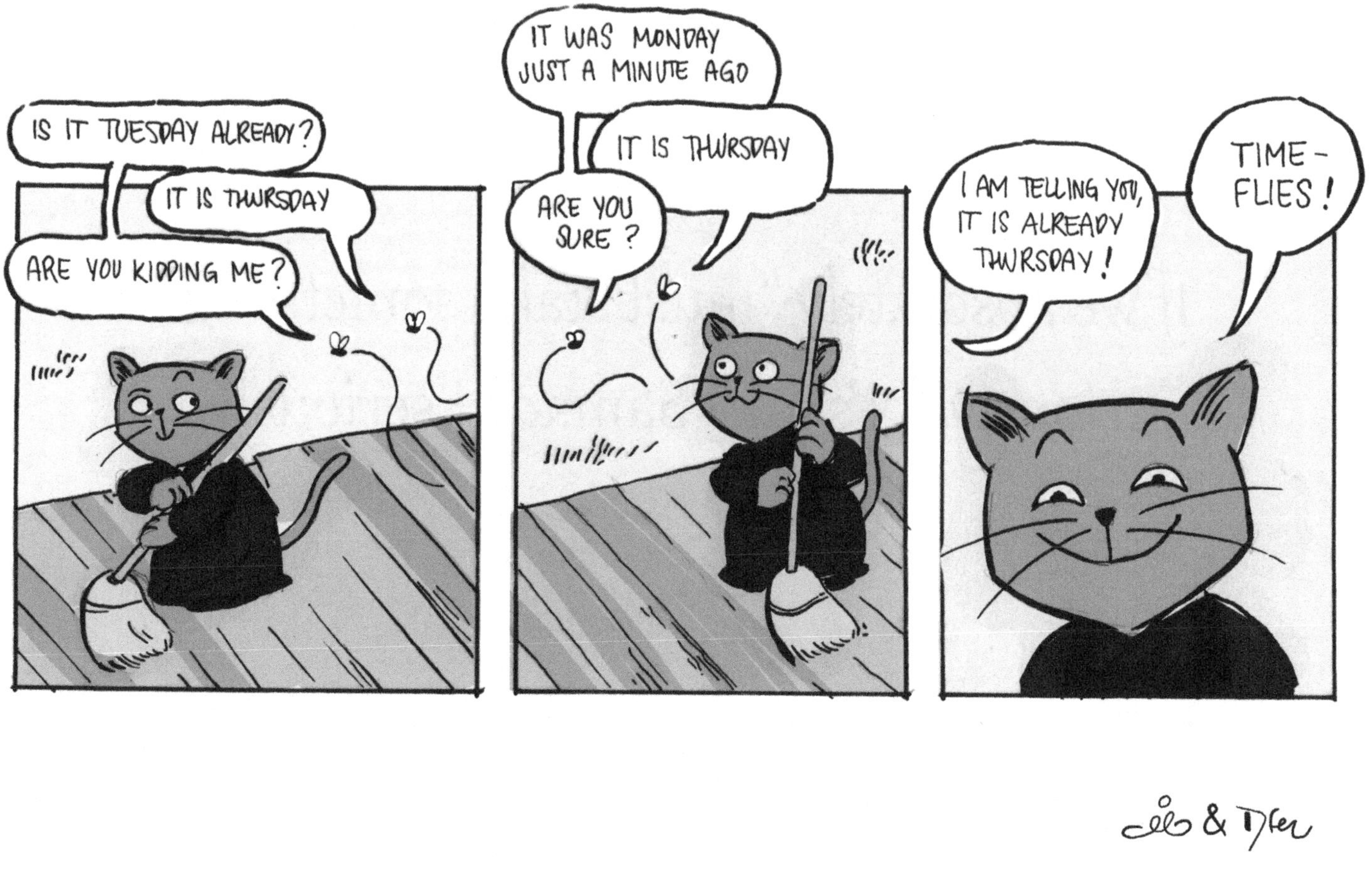

IS IT TUESDAY ALREADY?
IT IS THURSDAY
ARE YOU KIDDING ME?
IT WAS MONDAY JUST A MINUTE AGO
IT IS THURSDAY
ARE YOU SURE?
I AM TELLING YOU, IT IS ALREADY THURSDAY!
TIME-FLIES!

If we absolutely "must" take something seriously, let's take Samadhi seriously.

Camp

SAY TOBI... ARE YOU COMING TO SUMMER CAMP IN THE TEMPLE THIS YEAR?
OH, I DONT KNOW CHUCK. IT ALL SOUNDS A BIT FASCIST TO ME. ALL THOSE ARBITRARY RULES, RITUALS, CHORES... I DON'T KNOW
NAH! THE SUMMER CAMP IS JUST A TIME AND PLACE WHERE WE INTENSIVELY PRACTICE OUR CONCENTRATION
OH, YOU MEAN A "CONCENTRATION" CAMP?

So you want patience? You go-getter you!
What are you waiting for?

Kate

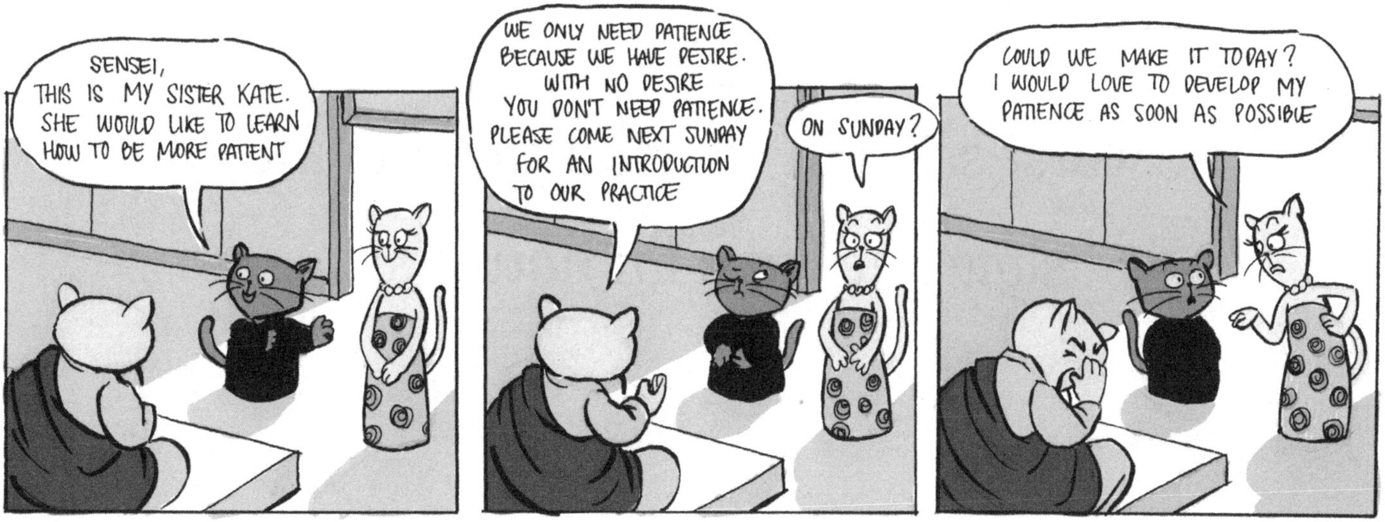
SENSEI, THIS IS MY SISTER KATE. SHE WOULD LIKE TO LEARN HOW TO BE MORE PATIENT
WE ONLY NEED PATIENCE BECAUSE WE HAVE DESIRE. WITH NO DESIRE YOU DON'T NEED PATIENCE. PLEASE COME NEXT SUNDAY FOR AN INTRODUCTION TO OUR PRACTICE
ON SUNDAY?
COULD WE MAKE IT TODAY? I WOULD LOVE TO DEVELOP MY PATIENCE AS SOON AS POSSIBLE

The worst sand in your butt is the fine and slow one from an hourglass.

Patience

SO YOU SIT LIKE THIS, FOCUS ON YOUR BREATHING AND WATCH YOUR THOUGHTS. THIS IS A GOOD WAY TO DEVELOP PATIENCE, OK?
OK.
AND?!

There is no paradox:
Everything I say is a lie.

Lunch

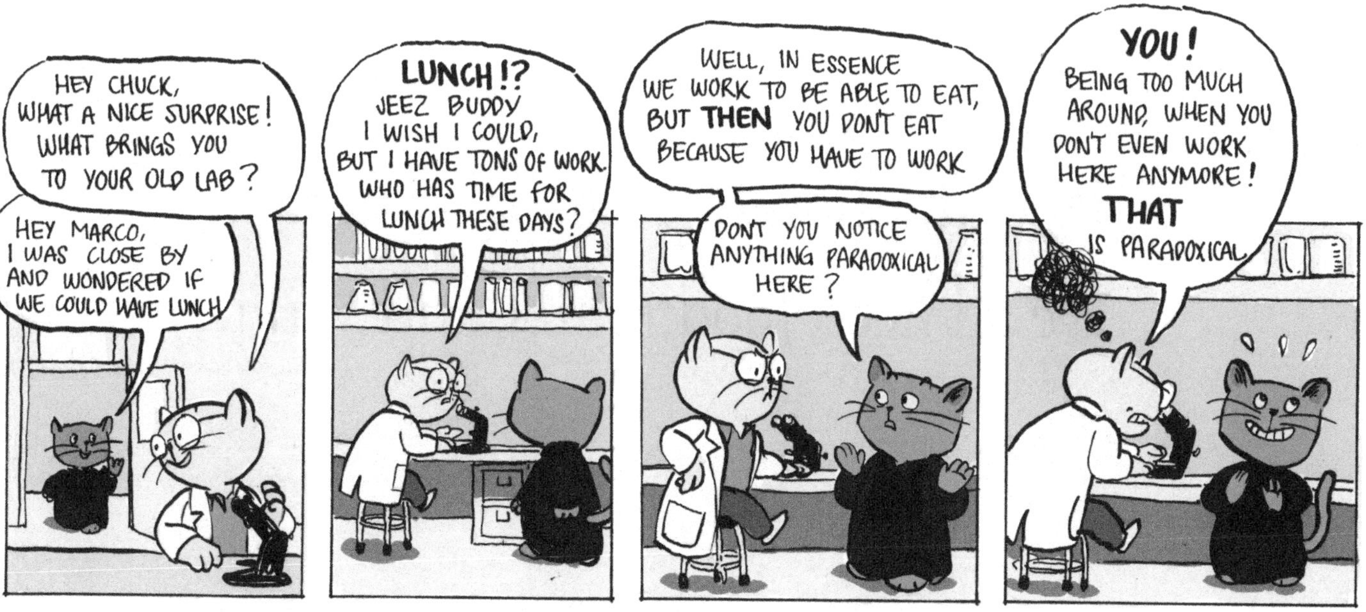
HEY CHUCK, WHAT A NICE SURPRISE! WHAT BRINGS YOU TO YOUR OLD LAB?
HEY MARCO, I WAS CLOSE BY AND WONDERED IF WE COULD HAVE LUNCH
LUNCH!? JEEZ BUDDY I WISH I COULD, BUT I HAVE TONS OF WORK. WHO HAS TIME FOR LUNCH THESE DAYS?
WELL, IN ESSENCE WE WORK TO BE ABLE TO EAT, BUT THEN YOU DON'T EAT BECAUSE YOU HAVE TO WORK
DON'T YOU NOTICE ANYTHING PARADOXICAL HERE?
YOU! BEING TOO MUCH AROUND, WHEN YOU DON'T EVEN WORK HERE ANYMORE! THAT IS PARADOXICAL

Pay attention to your basic needs.
We all need food, water and WiFi.

Work

YOU KNOW... WE DON'T WORK ONLY FOR FOOD, THERE IS PERSONAL FULFILLMENT, DEVELOPMENT, GROWTH, SELF REALIZATION, DEVOTION, PASSION, SOCIAL AND ECONOMIC EXCHANGE...
RESPONSIBILITY, JOY, STATUS, FAME, FORTUNE, RECOGNITION, ACCEPTANCE, MATERIAL DESIRES, BOREDOM, OR EVEN CIRCUMVENTING THE VOID OF EXISTENCE !! IT'S NOT ONLY ABOUT FOOD !!
FINE. BUT YOU DON'T GET ANY OF THOSE IF YOU DON'T EAT, DO YOU ?
SOMBHIMG ISF MIFFING, THORE ISF NO SJCREEN IM FROND OFJ MY FJACE TJHIS ISF WEYRD...
JUST CHOKE SLOWER ON THAT SAD SANDWICH, YOU STILL HAVE 2 MINUTES

I would give my honest opinion,
but who am I to judge stupidity?

Judging

SENSEI! SENSEI! I CAN'T WORK WITH THEM! THEY DON'T KNOW HOW TO
CHUCK! PLEASE STOP JUDGING
ILL PERCEPTION OF OTHERS ONLY STRENGTHENS THE ILLUSION OF YOUR VIRTUES. CHOOSE SELF-EXPLORATION OVER CRITICIZING OTHERS
YES, SENSEI
THAT IS THE IDIOT I WAS TELLING YOU ABOUT
TSK TSK

Merrily, gently, down the stream...
But we better row!

Oyster

SPONTANEITY IS ESSENTIAL BUT VOLITION IS ALSO VITAL...
WE NEED AN EGO IN ORDER TO REALIZE THERE IS NO EGO...
TAKE AN OYSTER FOR EXAMPLE: BEAUTIFUL IMMOBILITY, A PEARL OF WISDOM INSIDE, BUT IT FLOWS ONLY WHERE THE CURRENT TAKES IT
THE OYSTER WILL **NEVER** REALIZE SATORI
BECAUSE IT'S TOO "SHELLFISH"
BECAUSE IT LACKS DETERMINATION!

You don't need to steal it.
I will relinquish my heart for you.

Cow

...SO I GREW UP IN THE CITY. THAT IS WHY I FIND SO WONDERFUL ALL THIS NATURE SURROUNDING THE MONASTERY
YEAH, IT'S REALLY SOMETHING, ISN'T IT?
HEY LOOK! HOW COME THAT COW HAS ONLY ONE UDDER?
WHICH ONE?
THAT ONE
THAT IS A VERY SPECIAL KIND OF COW...
IT'S CALLED "A BULL"

Fighting both expectation and memory,
he inhabits a fake present in the trap of
literal Dharma. Temple's vigilante, little brown
noser with a Zen master complex
(not judging, just saying):
My dear, dear friend: Henri Musan.

Present

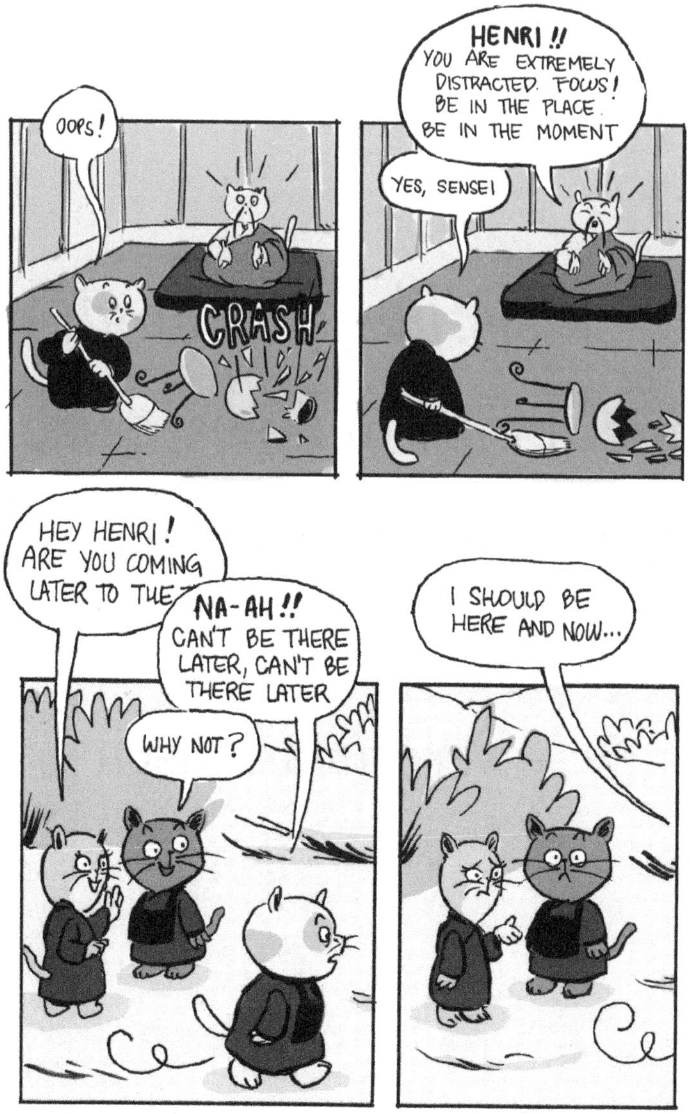
OOPS!
CRASH
HENRI!! YOU ARE EXTREMELY DISTRACTED. FOCUS! BE IN THE PLACE. BE IN THE MOMENT
YES, SENSEI
HEY HENRI! ARE YOU COMING LATER TO THE
NA-AH!! CAN'T BE THERE LATER, CAN'T BE THERE LATER
WHY NOT?
I SHOULD BE HERE AND NOW...

Tools, like our mind,
find merit only in how we use them.
It is dangerous when they use us instead.

– Verónica Llasca

Isolation

SO...DO YOU THINK TECHNOLOGY MIGHT SOMEDAY IMPROVE THE FEELING OF ISOLATION AND ALIENATION IN OUR CULTURES?
MHH...HARD TO SAY. I GUESS IT'S UP TO EACH INDIVIDUAL. EVEN IN CELL CULTURES
HERE, WE TRIED TO BIND NEURONS ALONG NANOCIRCUITS. MOST OF THE NEURONS USE THIS TECHNOLOGY TO CONNECT, TO COMMUNICATE AND SYNCHRONIZE WITH EACH OTHER
BUT TAKE A LOOK AT THIS ONE...
TOTALLY SURROUNDED BY OTHERS, AND STILL...
STRUGGLING WITH A CELL-FIE

What's with the crown?
Every branch is full of life
and blossoms with beauty.
Just sit and wait for the firemen.

Top

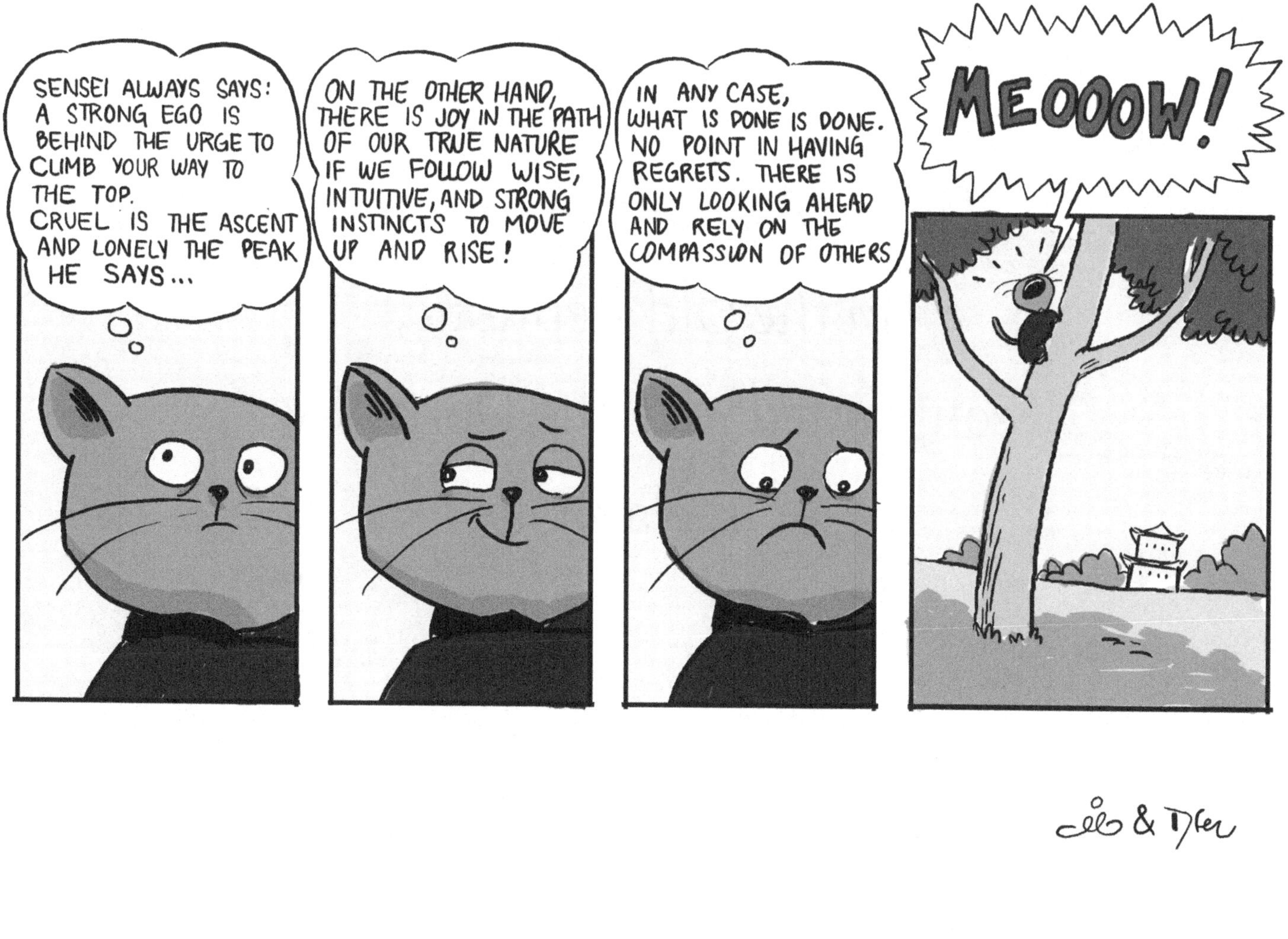
SENSEI ALWAYS SAYS: A STRONG EGO IS BEHIND THE URGE TO CLIMB YOUR WAY TO THE TOP. CRUEL IS THE ASCENT AND LONELY THE PEAK HE SAYS...
ON THE OTHER HAND, THERE IS JOY IN THE PATH OF OUR TRUE NATURE IF WE FOLLOW WISE, INTUITIVE, AND STRONG INSTINCTS TO MOVE UP AND RISE!
IN ANY CASE, WHAT IS DONE IS DONE. NO POINT IN HAVING REGRETS. THERE IS ONLY LOOKING AHEAD AND RELY ON THE COMPASSION OF OTHERS
MEOOOW!

Diego: A guardian of peace
in the Old Republic,
confronted with the Dark Side
of freelancing.

Force

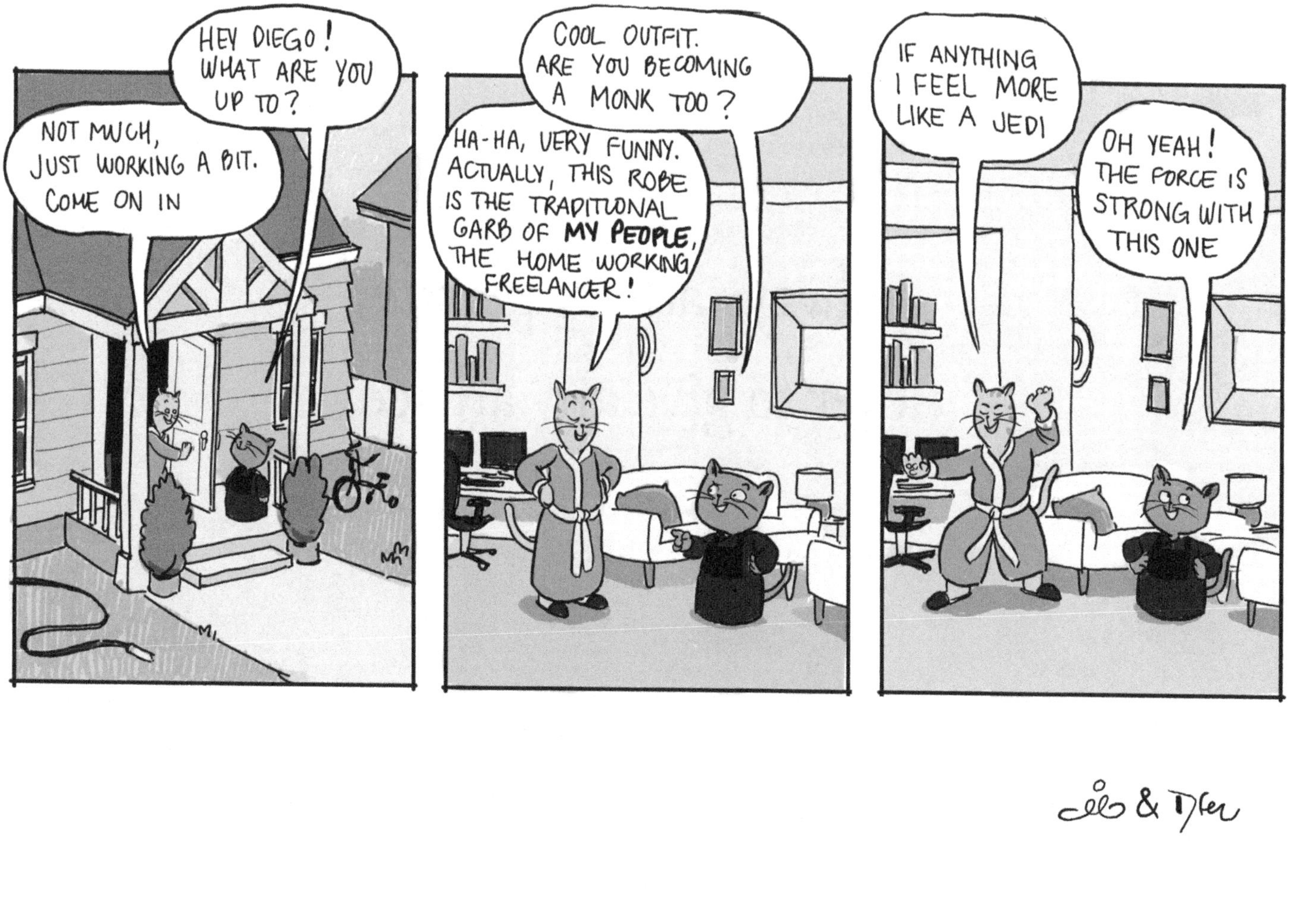
HEY DIEGO! WHAT ARE YOU UP TO?
NOT MUCH, JUST WORKING A BIT. COME ON IN
COOL OUTFIT. ARE YOU BECOMING A MONK TOO?
HA-HA, VERY FUNNY. ACTUALLY, THIS ROBE IS THE TRADITIONAL GARB OF **MY PEOPLE**, THE HOME WORKING FREELANCER!
IF ANYTHING I FEEL MORE LIKE A JEDI
OH YEAH! THE FORCE IS STRONG WITH THIS ONE

I always advise people
never to give any advice!

Depth

SO... HOW IS IT GOING WITH THAT CORPORATE LOGO YOU WERE WORKING ON?
WELL, NOT TOO BAD, BUT I AM A BIT WORRIED ABOUT DEPTH AND PERSPECTIVE
I KNOW HOW YOU FEEL... WORKING SO HARD FOR A FRIVOLOUS CORPORATION THAT MERCHANDISES USELESS ITEMS MIGHT LEAVE YOU WITH A SHALLOWNESS FEELING AND A LACK OF MEANING
BUT HEY! YOU HAVE KIDS AND...
OH! YOU MEAN IN THE **LOGO DESIGN**
THANKS MAN! I FEEL A LOT BETTER NOW

I think Sensei is sharpening his
claws on that tree that fell in the forest
and nobody heard.

Finger

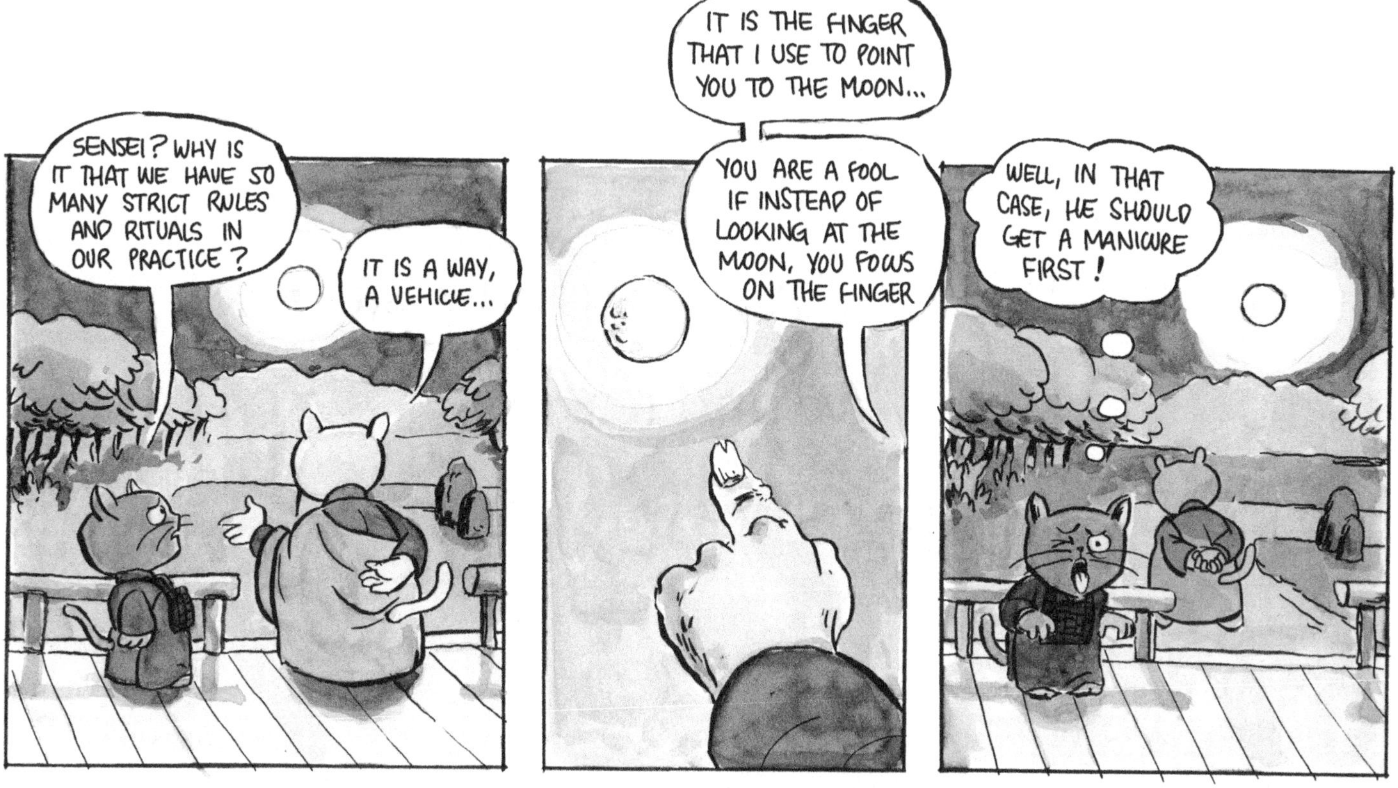
SENSEI? WHY IS IT THAT WE HAVE SO MANY STRICT RULES AND RITUALS IN OUR PRACTICE?
IT IS A WAY, A VEHICLE...
IT IS THE FINGER THAT I USE TO POINT YOU TO THE MOON...
YOU ARE A FOOL IF INSTEAD OF LOOKING AT THE MOON, YOU FOCUS ON THE FINGER
WELL, IN THAT CASE, HE SHOULD GET A MANICURE FIRST!

There is a reason why we say
"live and learn",
not the other way around.

Beauty

so...when done from the notion of a separated perceptive entity, direct realization of phenomena is an impossibility...
HEY CHUCK! A BUTTERFLY!
COULD YOU PLEASE FOCUS FOR A MINUTE BECKY?
WE ARE TRYING TO LEARN SOMETHING HERE!
OH! YOU MISSED IT!
IT WAS BREATHTAKING
CHAPTER III, opening consciousness to beauty awareness in daily life

Trying to find yourself?
Check the inner lost and found!

Stay

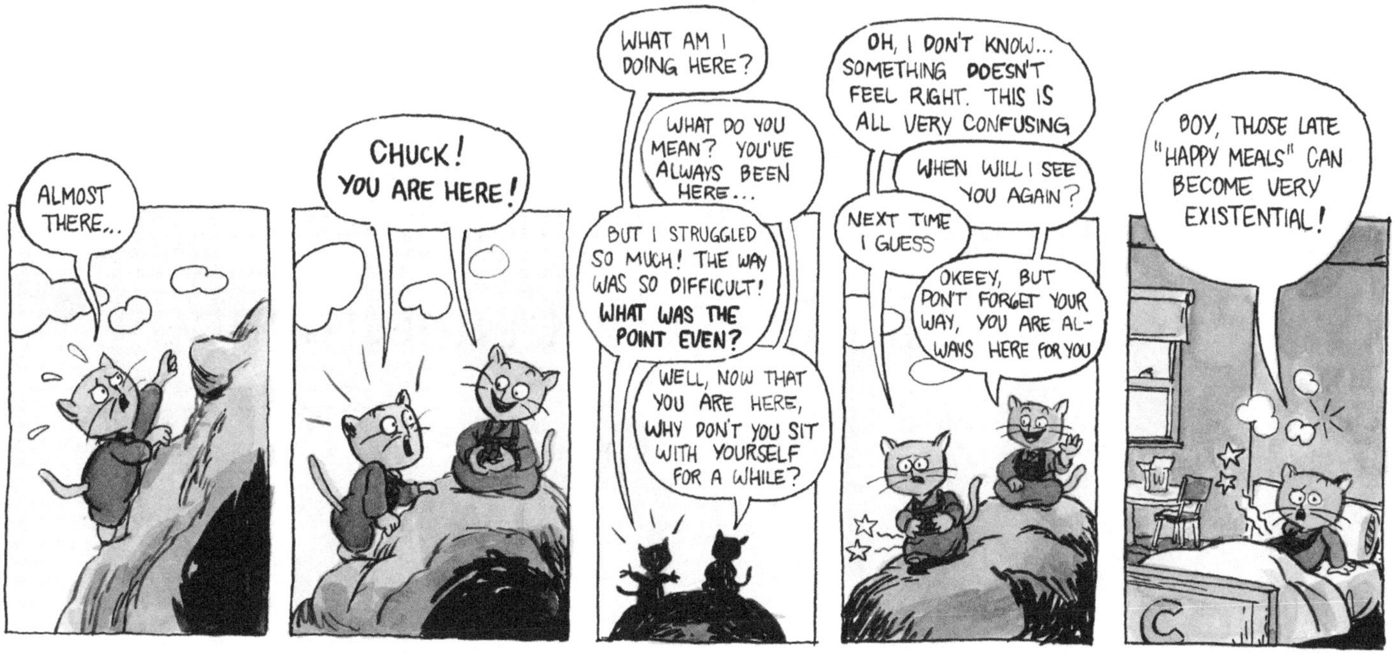
ALMOST THERE...
CHUCK! YOU ARE HERE!
WHAT AM I DOING HERE?
WHAT DO YOU MEAN? YOU'VE ALWAYS BEEN HERE...
BUT I STRUGGLED SO MUCH! THE WAY WAS SO DIFFICULT! WHAT WAS THE POINT EVEN?
WELL, NOW THAT YOU ARE HERE, WHY DON'T YOU SIT WITH YOURSELF FOR A WHILE?
OH, I DON'T KNOW... SOMETHING DOESN'T FEEL RIGHT. THIS IS ALL VERY CONFUSING
WHEN WILL I SEE YOU AGAIN?
NEXT TIME I GUESS
OKEEY, BUT DON'T FORGET YOUR WAY, YOU ARE AL-WAYS HERE FOR YOU
BOY, THOSE LATE "HAPPY MEALS" CAN BECOME VERY EXISTENTIAL!

When in doubt, get insurance.
You don't have to deal with uncertainty
these days.

Sure

ONE THING I CAN TELL YOU CHUCK, I AM NOT A MAN OF FAITH, I AM A SKEPTIC
YOU ARE A SKEPTIC
YES
ARE YOU?
YES, I AM
ARE YOU SURE?
COMPLETELY
LIKE, SURE SURE?
ABSOLUTELY, UNDENIABLY, POSITIVELY, NO DOUBT ABOUT IT, I AM A SKEPTIC!
WELL... YOU CERTAINLY SEEM TO HAVE A LOT OF FAITH IN YOUR SKEPTICISM!

The reason I belong to my tautology club is because I am on the member's list.

Believe

I AM A SKEPTIC BECAUSE I ONLY BELIEVE IN DEMONSTRATED FACTS
BUT YOU BELIEVE ONLY IN DEMONSTRATED FACTS BECAUSE YOU ARE A SKEPTIC...
CIRCULAR REASONING WORKS BECAUSE CIRCULAR REASONING WORKS
MAYBE YOU JUST BELIEVE THAT YOU ARE A SKEPTIC!
TAUTOLOGICAL FREAK!!

Practice... it does make perfect!!!

Practice

LOOK CHUCK, I KNOW IT'S DIFFICULT. THE FEAR, THE BURNING, THE BITTERNESS...
IT SEEMS IMPOSSIBLE AT THE BEGINNING AND YOU END UP SEEING A HALF EMPTY GLASS!
TRUST YOURSELF! IT IS A MATTER OF PRACTICE.
WITH DISCIPLINE AND TIME THE INITIAL SOURNESS BECOMES A JOYFUL AND MINDLESS STATE OF THE SPIRIT WHERE THAT HALF EMPTY GLASS IS NOT AN OPTION ANYMORE...
NOW DRINK UP YOUR **ENTIRE** SAKE AND QUIT BEING A WUSS!

At the lab, sometimes barometers are not enough to measure pressure.

Hand

CHUCK! EHMMM, LISTEN, IF YOU HAVE TIME, CAN YOU CHECK OUT SOME EXPERIMENTAL DATA? WE... MIGHT NEED A HAND IN THE LAB
SURE! GLAD I CAN HELP
SO, WHAT IS IT? ANOTHER SCIENTIFIC BREAKTHROUGH?
NOPE
ANOTHER SCIENTIFIC BREAKDOWN
PAPERS!
GRANTS!
GRANTS!
PAPERS!

To understand someone's inspiration,
you might require a deep exhalation.
Feel free to try it now.

Inspiration

THE END PRODUCT LOOKS SIMPLE, BUT THE CONCEPT TOOK YEARS TO DEVELOP. ULTIMATE INSPIRATION ARRIVED AT A LATE STAGE IN HIS LIFE
REALLY? WHEN?
AS HE STARTED LOOSING HAIR IN THE SHOWER

You have to think like a cat
to be free from the rat race.

Race

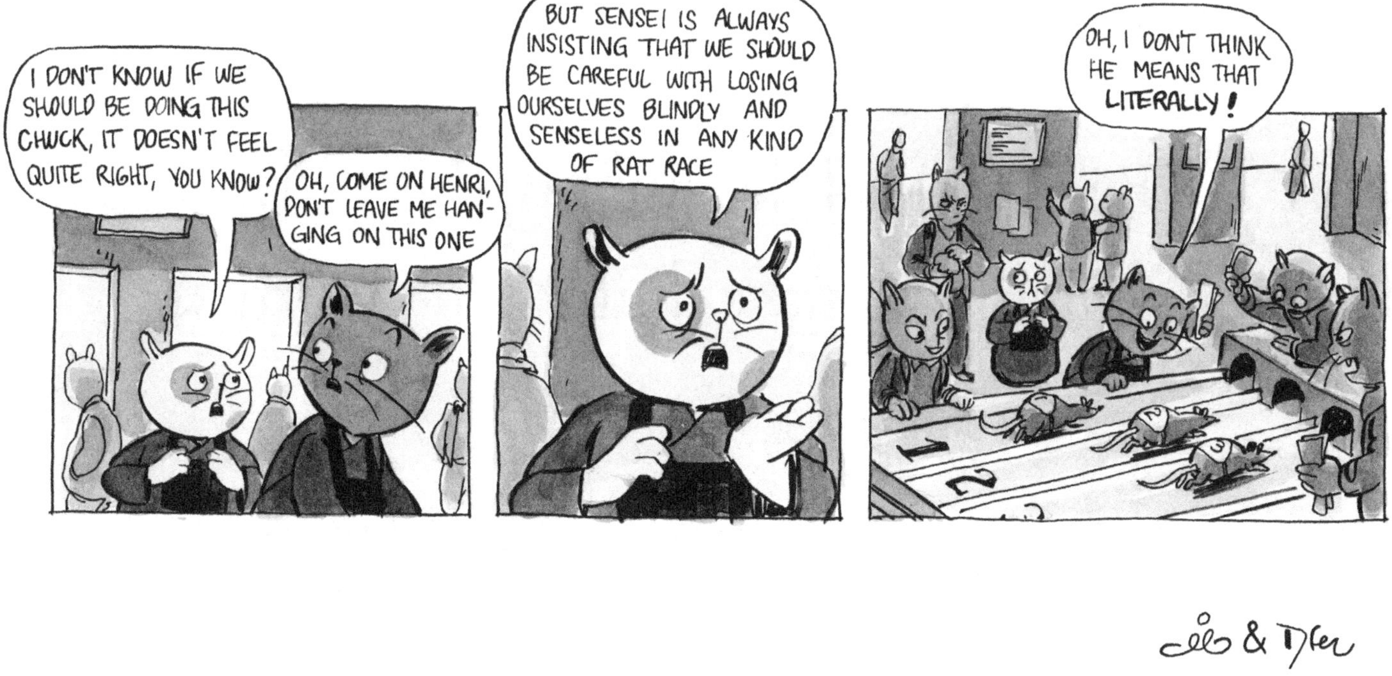
I DON'T KNOW IF WE SHOULD BE DOING THIS CHUCK, IT DOESN'T FEEL QUITE RIGHT, YOU KNOW?
OH, COME ON HENRI, DON'T LEAVE ME HANGING ON THIS ONE
BUT SENSEI IS ALWAYS INSISTING THAT WE SHOULD BE CAREFUL WITH LOSING OURSELVES BLINDLY AND SENSELESS IN ANY KIND OF RAT RACE
OH, I DON'T THINK HE MEANS THAT LITERALLY!
1
2

Be careful while rubbing this belly,
you might scare the fluttering butterflies.

Absence

GOOD BYE GUYS, SEE YOU SOON!
GOOD BYE BECKY !!
YOU KNOW HOW A PARADOX CAN BREAK YOUR MIND BUT AT THE SAME TIME MAKE SO MUCH SENSE?
YES, WHY?
EVERY TIME SHE GOES AWAY I AM **FILLED** WITH HER **ABSENCE**

Pay attention to the little things.
You will fall in love!

Car

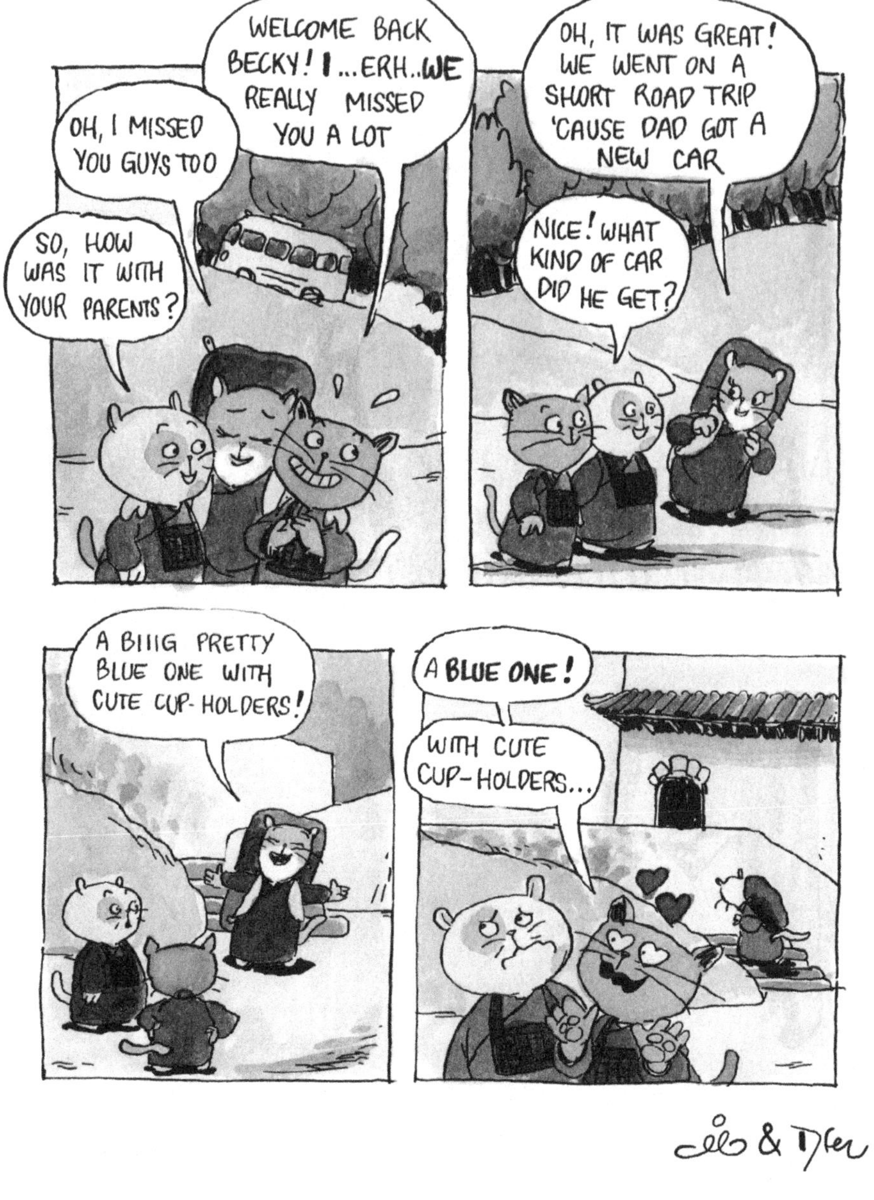
WELCOME BACK BECKY! I ...ERH..WE REALLY MISSED YOU A LOT
OH, I MISSED YOU GUYS TOO
SO, HOW WAS IT WITH YOUR PARENTS?
OH, IT WAS GREAT! WE WENT ON A SHORT ROAD TRIP 'CAUSE DAD GOT A NEW CAR
NICE! WHAT KIND OF CAR DID HE GET?
A BIIIG PRETTY BLUE ONE WITH CUTE CUP-HOLDERS!
A BLUE ONE!
WITH CUTE CUP-HOLDERS...

Melody, obviating solubility and sedimentation, is here to stir things (up).

Revolution

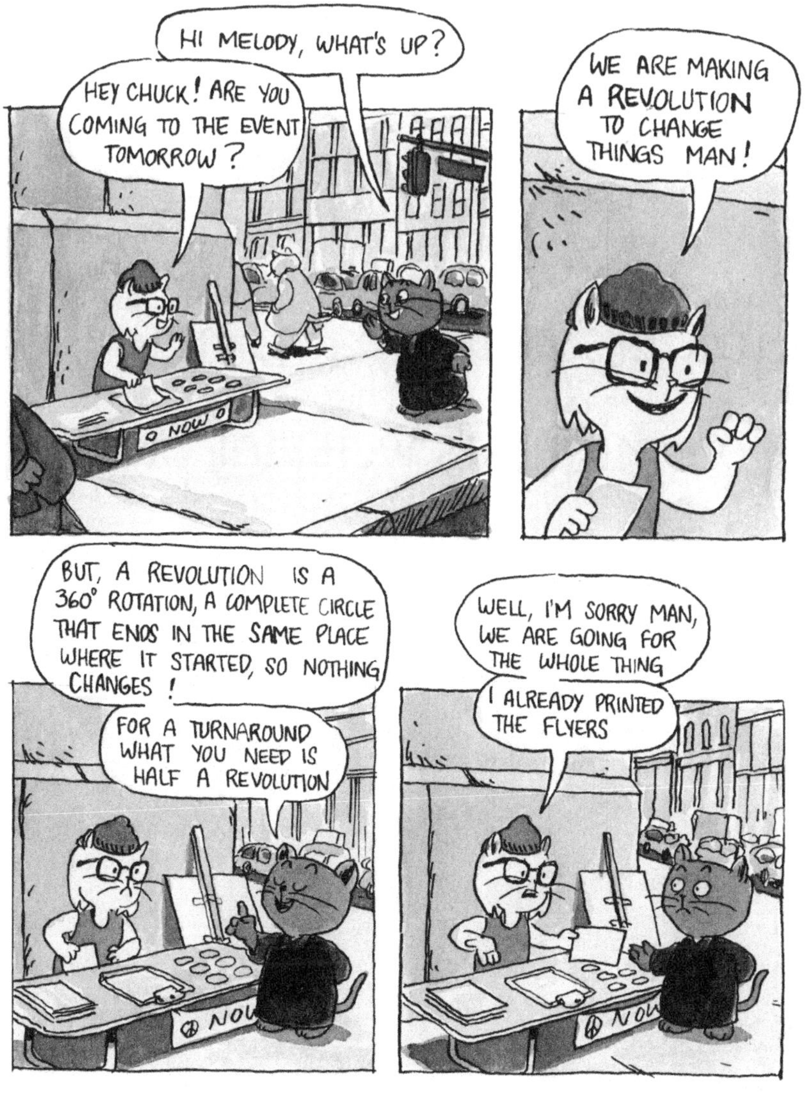
HEY CHUCK! ARE YOU COMING TO THE EVENT TOMORROW?
HI MELODY, WHAT'S UP?
WE ARE MAKING A REVOLUTION TO CHANGE THINGS MAN!
BUT, A REVOLUTION IS A 360° ROTATION, A COMPLETE CIRCLE THAT ENDS IN THE SAME PLACE WHERE IT STARTED, SO NOTHING CHANGES!
FOR A TURNAROUND WHAT YOU NEED IS HALF A REVOLUTION
WELL, I'M SORRY MAN, WE ARE GOING FOR THE WHOLE THING
I ALREADY PRINTED THE FLYERS
NOW
NOW
NOW

If you understand a painting beforehand, you might as well not paint it.

— Salvador Dalí

Intellect

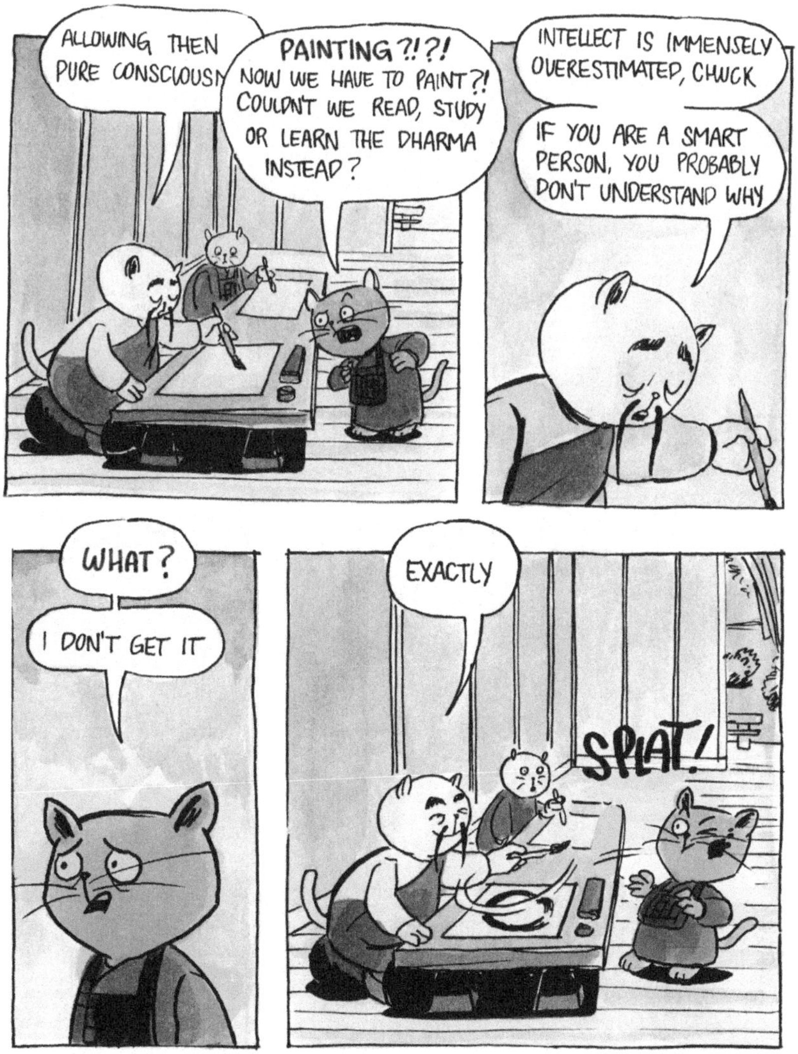
ALLOWING THEN PURE CONSCIOUSN
PAINTING?!?!
NOW WE HAVE TO PAINT?! COULDN'T WE READ, STUDY OR LEARN THE DHARMA INSTEAD?
INTELLECT IS IMMENSELY OVERESTIMATED, CHUCK
IF YOU ARE A SMART PERSON, YOU PROBABLY DON'T UNDERSTAND WHY
WHAT?
I DON'T GET IT
EXACTLY
SPLAT!

Jeb & Tyler

I don't see what is wrong with resting...
Especially if it is in peace!

Break

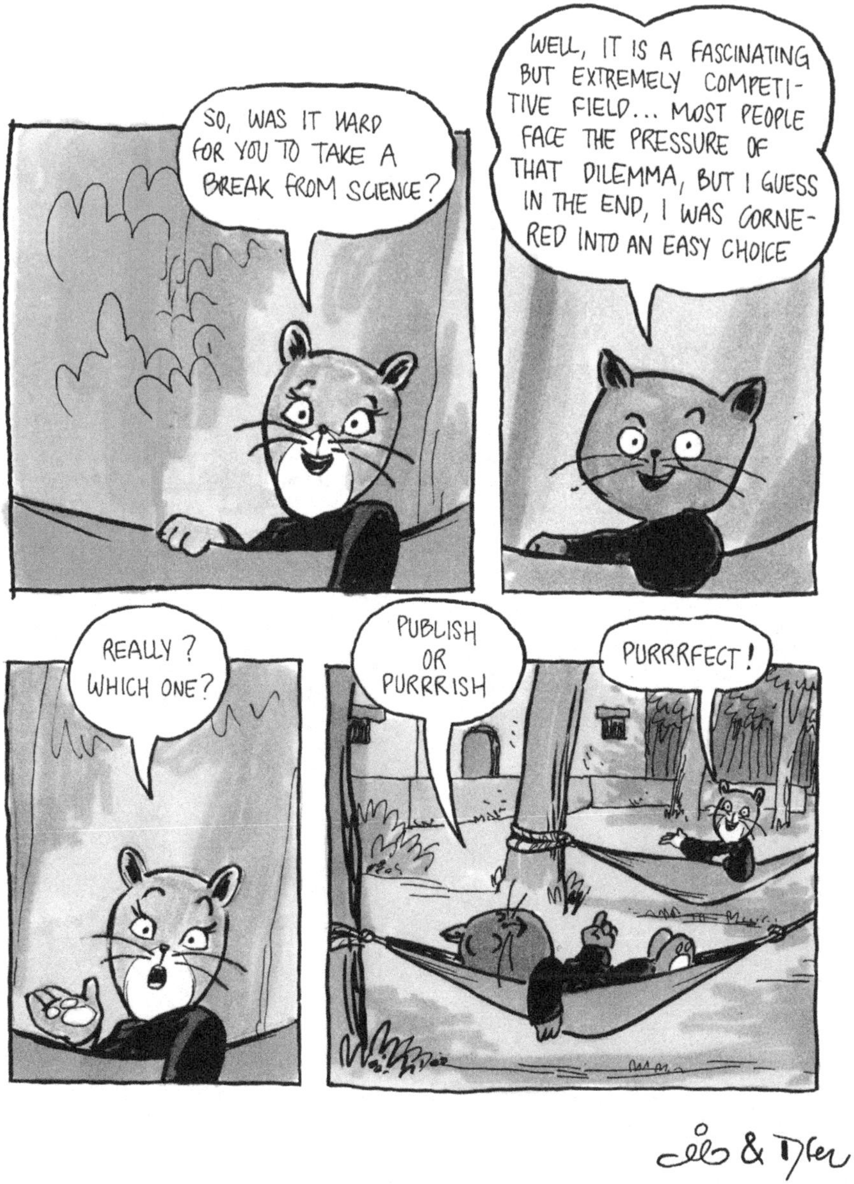
SO, WAS IT HARD FOR YOU TO TAKE A BREAK FROM SCIENCE?
WELL, IT IS A FASCINATING BUT EXTREMELY COMPETI-TIVE FIELD... MOST PEOPLE FACE THE PRESSURE OF THAT DILEMMA, BUT I GUESS IN THE END, I WAS CORNE-RED INTO AN EASY CHOICE
REALLY? WHICH ONE?
PUBLISH OR PURRRISH
PURRRFECT!

We don't need a passport to go
beyond the borders of our mind.

– Carlos Valencia

Lines

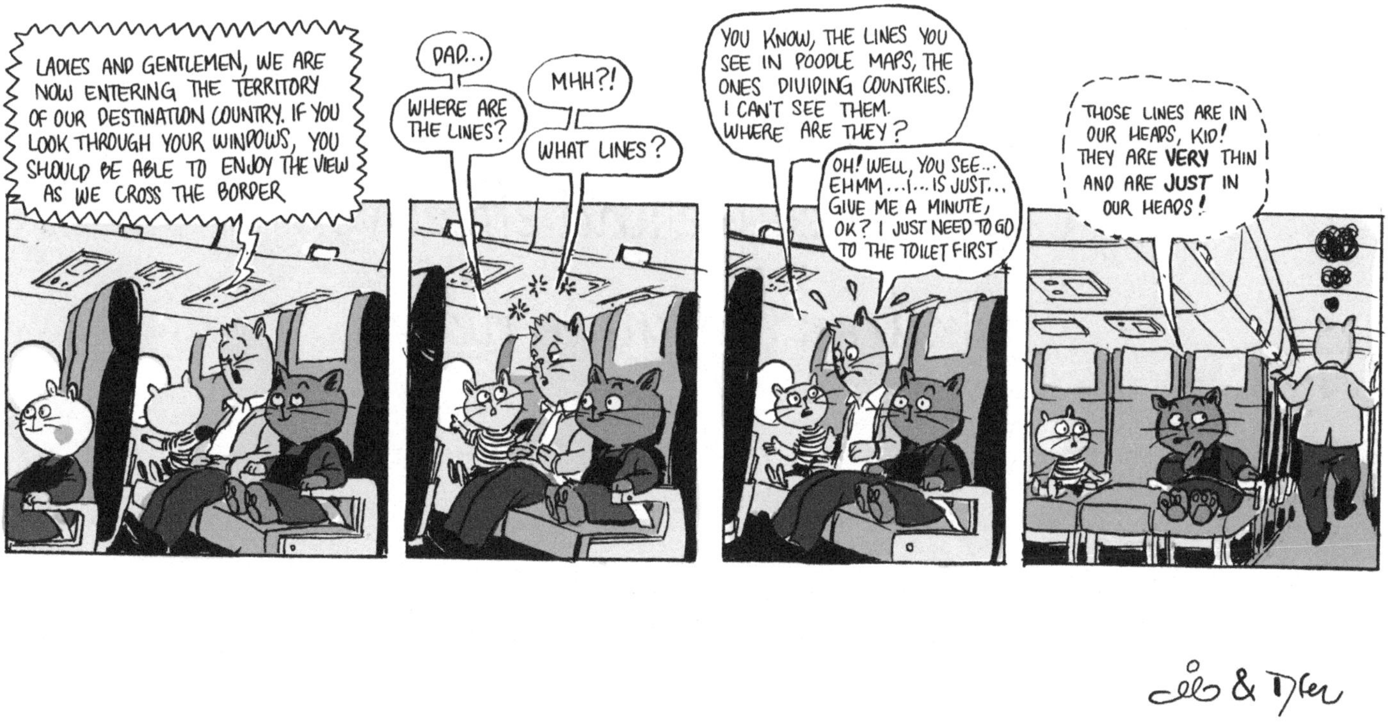
LADIES AND GENTLEMEN, WE ARE NOW ENTERING THE TERRITORY OF OUR DESTINATION COUNTRY. IF YOU LOOK THROUGH YOUR WINDOWS, YOU SHOULD BE ABLE TO ENJOY THE VIEW AS WE CROSS THE BORDER
DAD...
WHERE ARE THE LINES?
MHH?!
WHAT LINES?
YOU KNOW, THE LINES YOU SEE IN POODLE MAPS, THE ONES DIVIDING COUNTRIES. I CAN'T SEE THEM. WHERE ARE THEY?
OH! WELL, YOU SEE... EHMM...I...IS JUST... GIVE ME A MINUTE, OK? I JUST NEED TO GO TO THE TOILET FIRST
THOSE LINES ARE IN OUR HEADS, KID! THEY ARE VERY THIN AND ARE JUST IN OUR HEADS!

Clear, reflective and effective:
Indra's mosquito net.

Mosquitoes

...AND THESE ARE OUR DWELLINGS. WE FOREST MONKS FOLLOW BUDDHA'S LIFESTYLE AND PRACTICE IN THE WOODS
AMAZING, BUT...
WHAT DO YOU DO ABOUT MOSQUITOES AROUND HERE?
SCRATCH SCRATCH
WELL, WE RESPECT ALL LIFE SO WE TRY TO KEEP THEM AWAY WITH SMOKE, CREAMS, NETS, OILS, INCENSE, POMADES FRAGRANCES, LOTIONS, OINTMENTS!
EHMM... YEAH!
ESPECIALLY LOVING KINDNESS
AND LOVING KINDNESS

Birds dress in mating feathers,
blossoms stand proudly on each branch, and
the wind plays gently with the grass.
Suddenly the masked dancer
sprouts from the carnival.
What is not natural about spring?

— So Kai

Natural

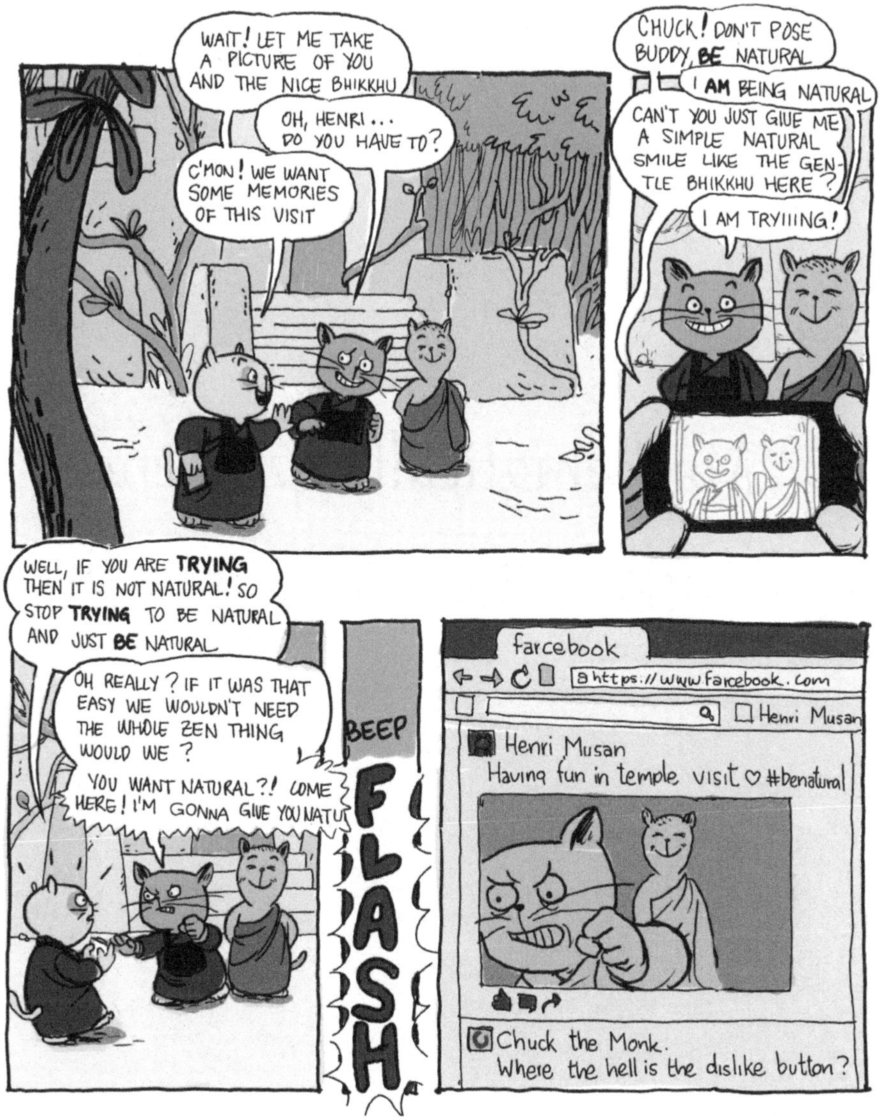
WAIT! LET ME TAKE A PICTURE OF YOU AND THE NICE BHIKKHU
OH, HENRI... DO YOU HAVE TO?
C'MON! WE WANT SOME MEMORIES OF THIS VISIT
CHUCK! DON'T POSE BUDDY, BE NATURAL
I AM BEING NATURAL
CAN'T YOU JUST GIVE ME A SIMPLE NATURAL SMILE LIKE THE GENTLE BHIKKHU HERE?
I AM TRYIIING!
WELL, IF YOU ARE TRYING THEN IT IS NOT NATURAL! SO STOP TRYING TO BE NATURAL AND JUST BE NATURAL
OH REALLY? IF IT WAS THAT EASY WE WOULDN'T NEED THE WHOLE ZEN THING WOULD WE?
YOU WANT NATURAL?! COME HERE! I'M GONNA GIVE YOU NATU
BEEP
FLASH
farcebook
https://www.farcebook.com
Henri Musan
Henri Musan
Having fun in temple visit ♡ #benatural
Chuck the Monk.
Where the hell is the dislike button?

Mathematically: |Absence|

Besides... It is always positive!

Absolute

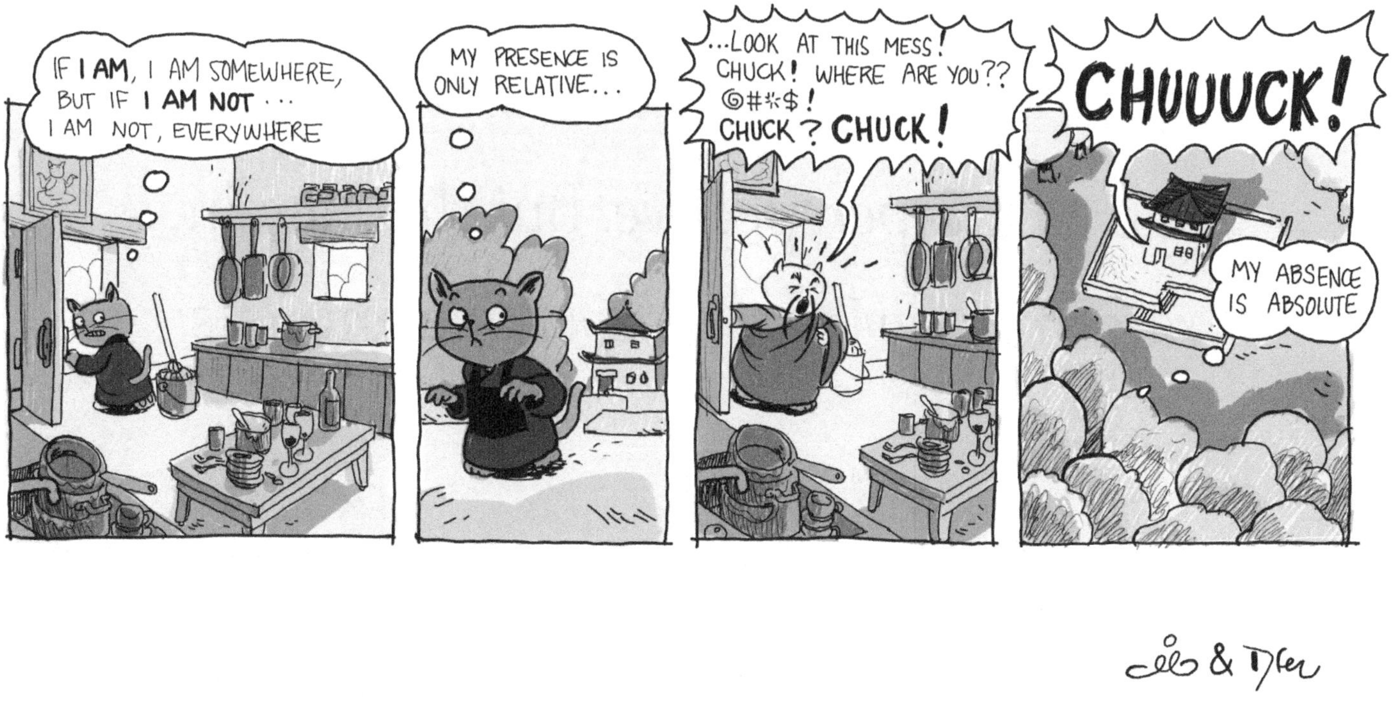

IF I AM, I AM SOMEWHERE, BUT IF I AM NOT ... I AM NOT, EVERYWHERE
MY PRESENCE IS ONLY RELATIVE...
...LOOK AT THIS MESS! CHUCK! WHERE ARE YOU?? @#*$! CHUCK? CHUCK!
CHUUUCK!
MY ABSENCE IS ABSOLUTE

Such a low perspective. But then again, rats are crawling, competitive animals.

Strive

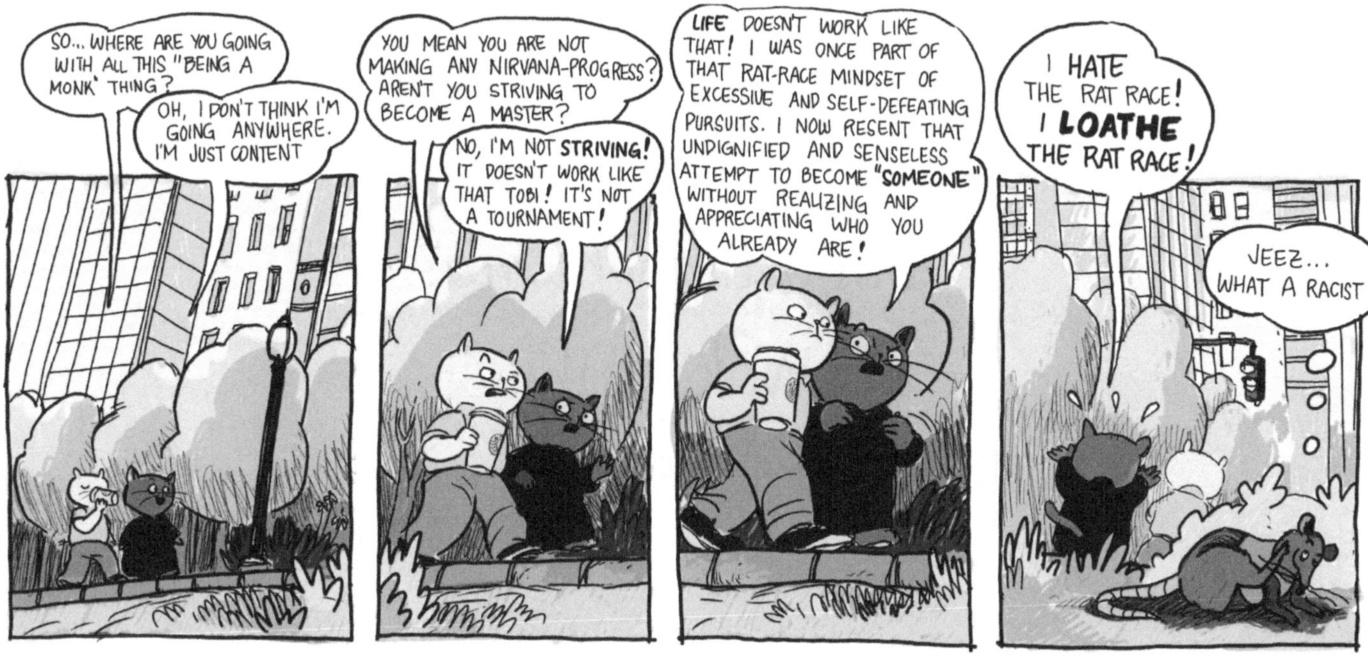
SO... WHERE ARE YOU GOING WITH ALL THIS "BEING A MONK" THING?
OH, I DON'T THINK I'M GOING ANYWHERE. I'M JUST CONTENT
YOU MEAN YOU ARE NOT MAKING ANY NIRVANA-PROGRESS? AREN'T YOU STRIVING TO BECOME A MASTER?
NO, I'M NOT STRIVING! IT DOESN'T WORK LIKE THAT TOBI! IT'S NOT A TOURNAMENT!
LIFE DOESN'T WORK LIKE THAT! I WAS ONCE PART OF THAT RAT-RACE MINDSET OF EXCESSIVE AND SELF-DEFEATING PURSUITS. I NOW RESENT THAT UNDIGNIFIED AND SENSELESS ATTEMPT TO BECOME "SOMEONE" WITHOUT REALIZING AND APPRECIATING WHO YOU ALREADY ARE!
I HATE THE RAT RACE! I LOATHE THE RAT RACE!
JEEZ... WHAT A RACIST

Comfortably numb?
Wake up!

Asleep

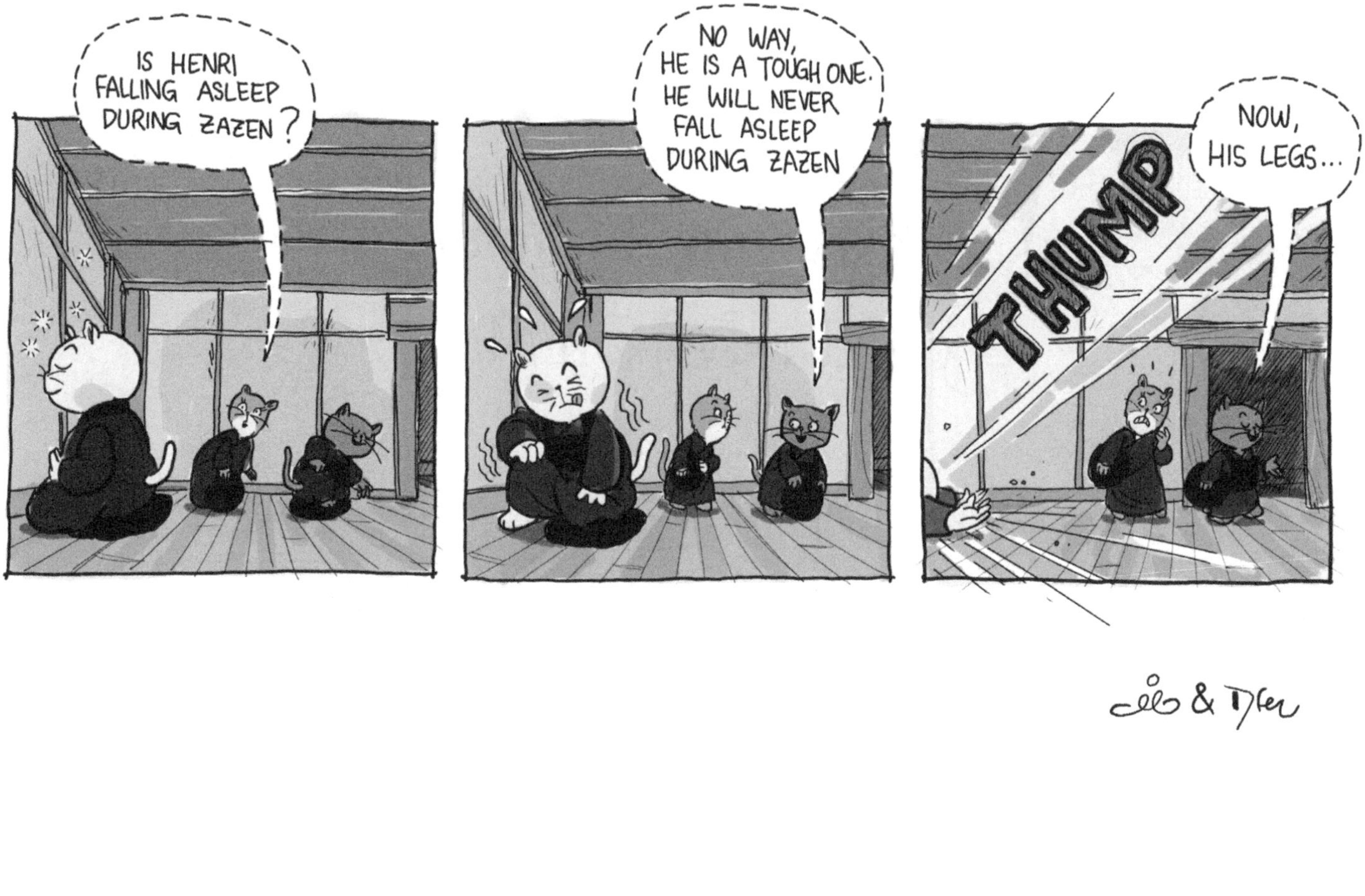
IS HENRI FALLING ASLEEP DURING ZAZEN?
NO WAY, HE IS A TOUGH ONE. HE WILL NEVER FALL ASLEEP DURING ZAZEN
THUMP
NOW, HIS LEGS...

This is how, at home,
you can be Iron Man!

Ironing

IRONING, IRONING, IRONING...
I AM GOING TO GET OLD DOING ALL THESE MEANINGLESS TASKS
GETTING WRINKLY WHILE DOING THE IRONING
DO YOU SEE THE IRONY?

Sometimes, for different reasons,
we pray before meals.

Fearless

ARE WE SURE ABOUT THIS?
WELL, WE SHOULD BE COMPASSIONATE HENRI
BUT I AM AFRAID THE CONSEQUENCES MIGHT BE UNPREDICTABLE
OK, LISTEN TO ME...
WE ARE **MONKS**!
BAM
ABSOLUTE FREEDOM MEANS TO REMAIN **FEARLESS** IN THE ABSENCE OF CERTAINTY...
NOW PULL YOURSELVES TOGETHER AND SMILE!
DINNER IS REAAAAAADY!

Cats, no less liquid than their shadows,
offer no angles to the wind.
They slip, diminished, neat,
through loopholes less than themselves.

– A.S.J. Tessimond

Hope

OH MAN!
DO NOT DESIRE...
DO NOT REJECT...
BOY. I HOPE THAT INCLUDES NOT DESIRING REJECTION AND NOT REJECTING DESIRE

Solve the "Mayday Poppins" riddle.
Do the magic yourself!!!

Nanny

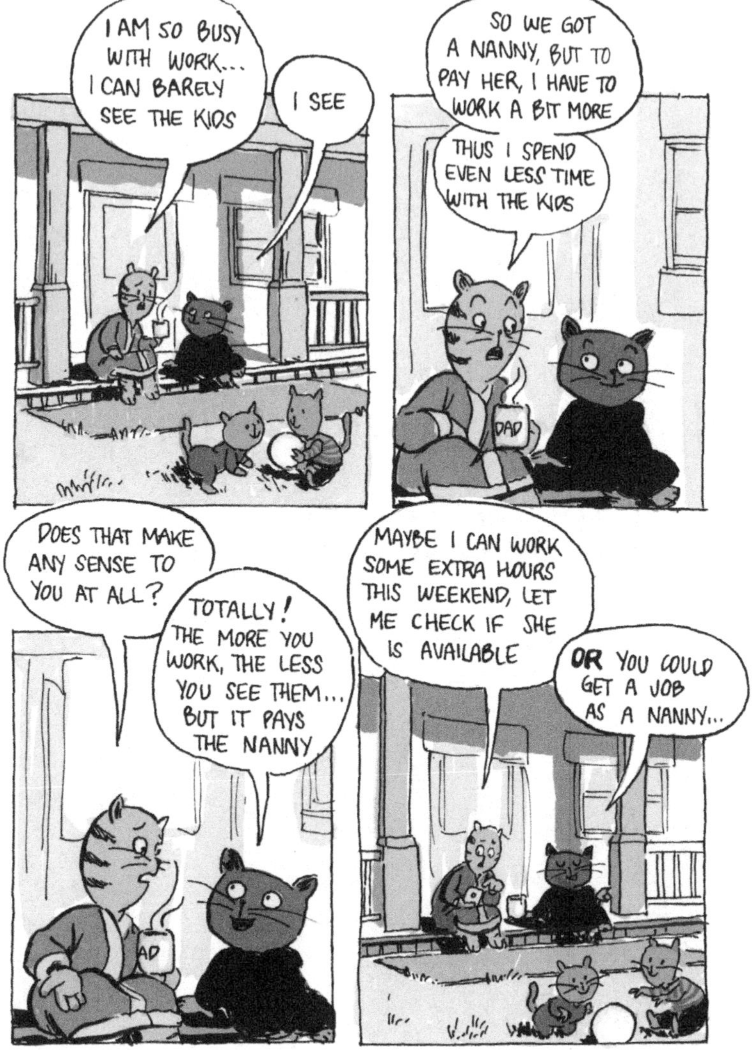
I AM SO BUSY WITH WORK... I CAN BARELY SEE THE KIDS
I SEE
SO WE GOT A NANNY, BUT TO PAY HER, I HAVE TO WORK A BIT MORE
THUS I SPEND EVEN LESS TIME WITH THE KIDS
DAD
DOES THAT MAKE ANY SENSE TO YOU AT ALL?
TOTALLY! THE MORE YOU WORK, THE LESS YOU SEE THEM... BUT IT PAYS THE NANNY
MAYBE I CAN WORK SOME EXTRA HOURS THIS WEEKEND, LET ME CHECK IF SHE IS AVAILABLE
OR YOU COULD GET A JOB AS A NANNY...

Illusion: In-Ludere (In play).
Chill out, it is only a game.

Illusions

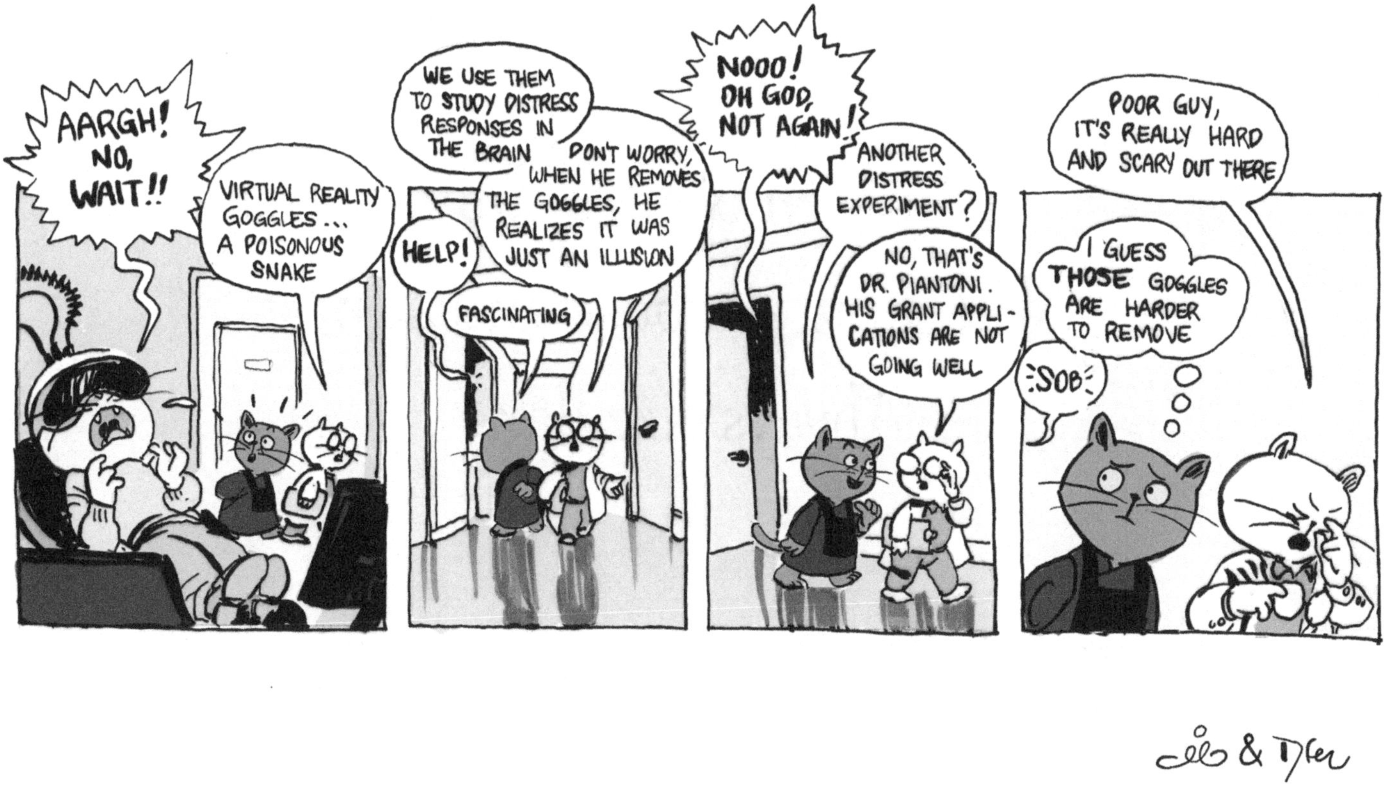
AARGH! NO, WAIT!!
VIRTUAL REALITY GOGGLES... A POISONOUS SNAKE
WE USE THEM TO STUDY DISTRESS RESPONSES IN THE BRAIN
DON'T WORRY, WHEN HE REMOVES THE GOGGLES, HE REALIZES IT WAS JUST AN ILLUSION
HELP!
FASCINATING
NOOO! OH GOD, NOT AGAIN!
ANOTHER DISTRESS EXPERIMENT?
NO, THAT'S DR. PIANTONI. HIS GRANT APPLI-CATIONS ARE NOT GOING WELL
POOR GUY, IT'S REALLY HARD AND SCARY OUT THERE
I GUESS THOSE GOGGLES ARE HARDER TO REMOVE
SOB

A pinch of meaning,
add some purpose and stir.
Always circular.

Soup

I AM SORRY CHUCK, I CAN'T GO TO THE MOVIES WITH YOU...
OH, OK. WHAT ARE YOU DOING?
JUST SLICING SOME VEGGIES
COOL! WHAT FOR?
TO MAKE A SOUP...
TO GET SOME ENERGY... TO GO TO WORK... TO EARN SOME MONEY... TO BUY SOME VEGGIES... TO SLICE THEM...
TO MAKE MORE SOUP
OH BOY! THAT SOUNDS LIKE A VERY TELEOLOGICAL SOUP
SO... IT'S GOING TO BE A WHILE BUDDY

Tired of chasing? For a fresh start,
turn around and go the other way.
Repeat if necessary.

Wheel

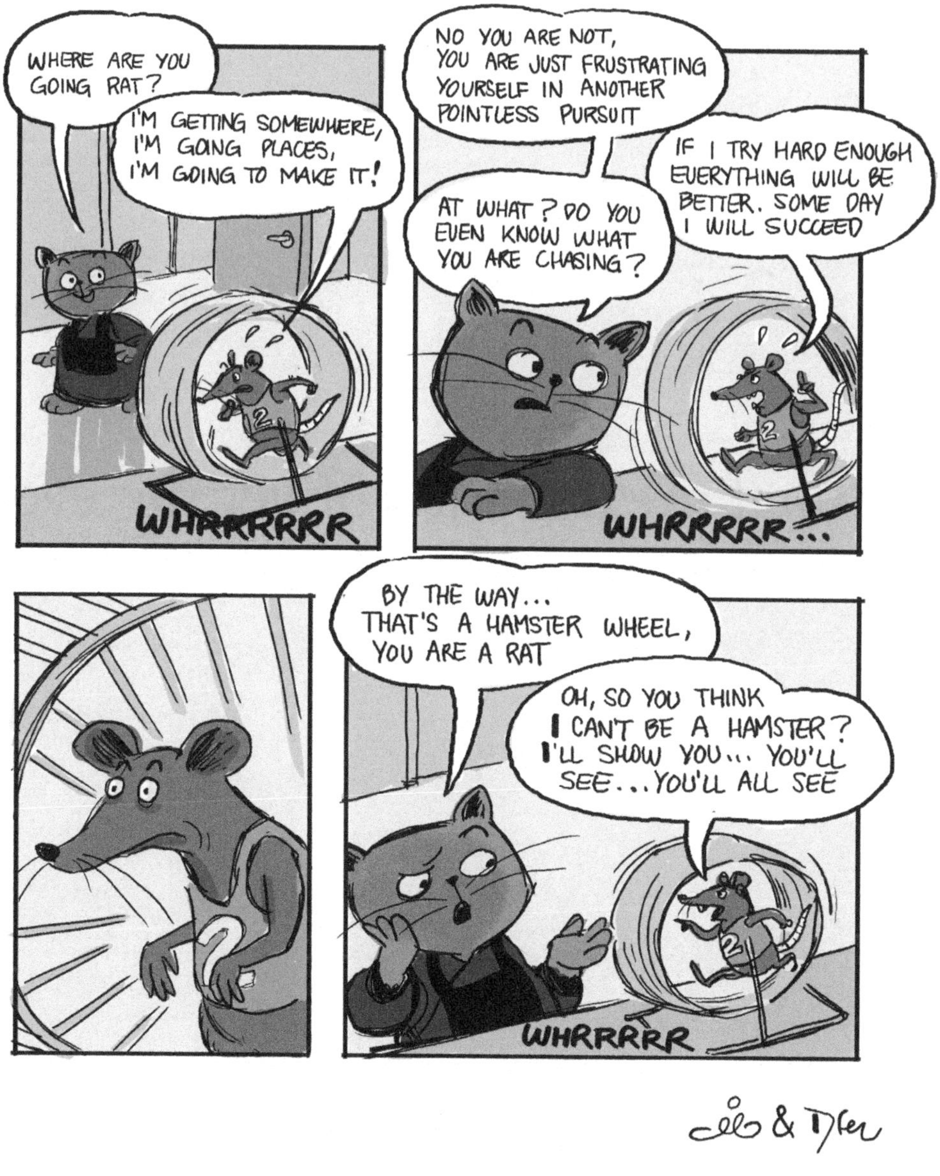
WHERE ARE YOU GOING RAT?
I'M GETTING SOMEWHERE, I'M GOING PLACES, I'M GOING TO MAKE IT!
WHRRRRRR
NO YOU ARE NOT, YOU ARE JUST FRUSTRATING YOURSELF IN ANOTHER POINTLESS PURSUIT
IF I TRY HARD ENOUGH EVERYTHING WILL BE BETTER. SOME DAY I WILL SUCCEED
AT WHAT? DO YOU EVEN KNOW WHAT YOU ARE CHASING?
WHRRRRR...
BY THE WAY... THAT'S A HAMSTER WHEEL, YOU ARE A RAT
OH, SO YOU THINK I CAN'T BE A HAMSTER? I'LL SHOW YOU... YOU'LL SEE... YOU'LL ALL SEE
WHRRRRR

What are the odds of getting even?

Bet

WHAT IS THIS?
YOU ARE GAMBLING!
AGAIN!!
YOU ARE SO WEAK CHUCK!
I BET YOU WILL NEVER GO BEYOND YOUR RISKY PASSIONS!!
DO YOU WANT TO MAKE IT INTERESTING?
$

Doubt sees the obstacles,
faith sees the way.

– Elizabeth Cheney

Worry

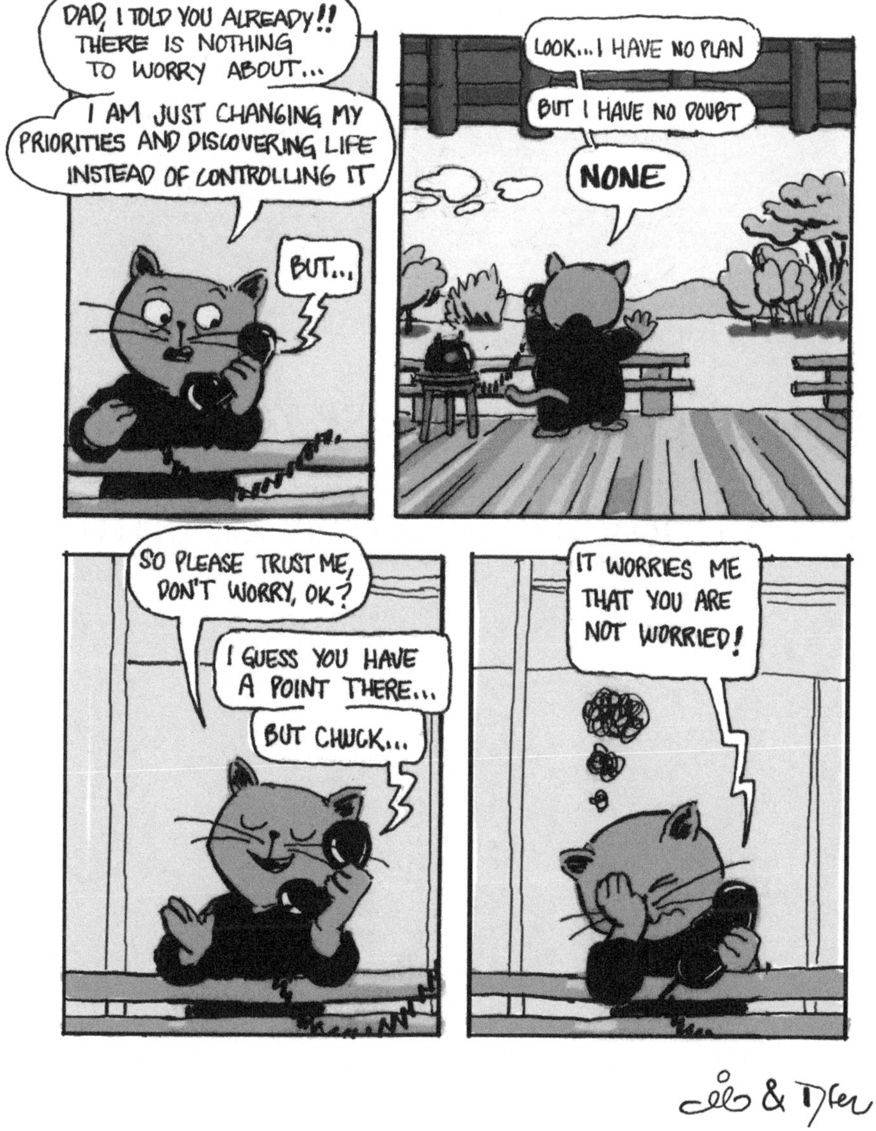
DAD, I TOLD YOU ALREADY!! THERE IS NOTHING TO WORRY ABOUT...
I AM JUST CHANGING MY PRIORITIES AND DISCOVERING LIFE INSTEAD OF CONTROLLING IT
BUT...
LOOK... I HAVE NO PLAN
BUT I HAVE NO DOUBT
NONE
SO PLEASE TRUST ME, DON'T WORRY, OK?
I GUESS YOU HAVE A POINT THERE...
BUT CHUCK...
IT WORRIES ME THAT YOU ARE NOT WORRIED!

Wrong crowd? Please read the room.
Nobody likes heresy in church.

Interested

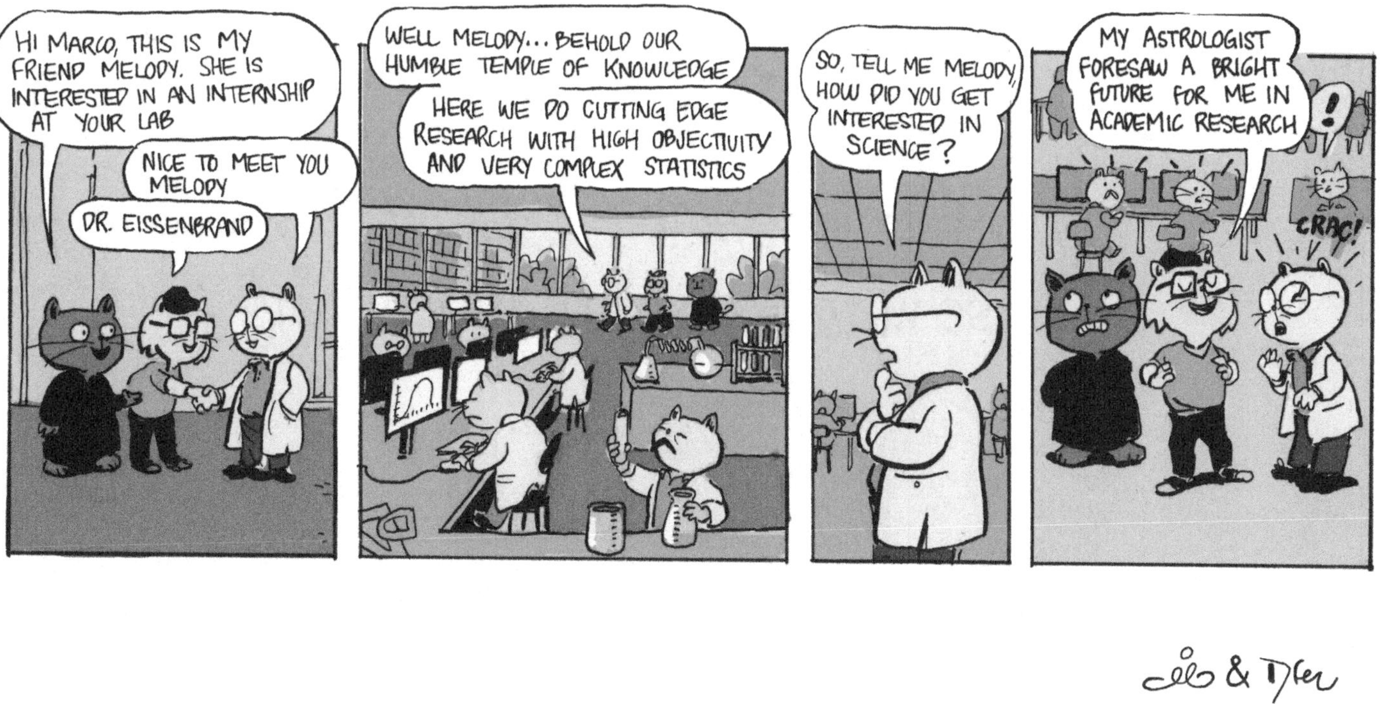

HI MARCO, THIS IS MY FRIEND MELODY. SHE IS INTERESTED IN AN INTERNSHIP AT YOUR LAB
NICE TO MEET YOU MELODY
DR. EISSENBRAND
WELL MELODY... BEHOLD OUR HUMBLE TEMPLE OF KNOWLEDGE
HERE WE DO CUTTING EDGE RESEARCH WITH HIGH OBJECTIVITY AND VERY COMPLEX STATISTICS
SO, TELL ME MELODY, HOW DID YOU GET INTERESTED IN SCIENCE?
MY ASTROLOGIST FORESAW A BRIGHT FUTURE FOR ME IN ACADEMIC RESEARCH
!
CRAC!

The little things are very strong
because we don't see them coming.

Balance

BZZZZZ
BZZZ...
PTAP
!
LITTLE THINGS STILL THROWING YOU OFF BALANCE?
ONLY THE VERY LITTLE

Sitting still in silence,
there are no answers.
Just truth.

– So Kai

Shikantaza

We hold and blow,
but it has to flow,
so we gladly bow,
and just let it go.

Essence

I AM REALLY IMPRESSED WITH THE TEMPLE. IT IS A TRUE SANCTUARY OF THE PRACTICE.
AND THE GARDEN... IT IS AN INTIMATE REFLECTION OF NATURE'S ESSENCE
THANKS. IT IS OUR HUMBLE TREASURE
HOWEVER, I AM VERY CURIOUS ABOUT THE ATYPICAL GARDEN FENCE
WELL, IT WASN'T PLANNED, BUT THE SAND ALSO EXALTS A LESS DESIRABLE ESSENCE OF OUR NATURE...
BEAR IN MIND, THIS IS MOSTLY A FELINE CONGREGATION

Nesting seminars, mating classes, flying workshops and singing contests.
The early bird gets the job.

City

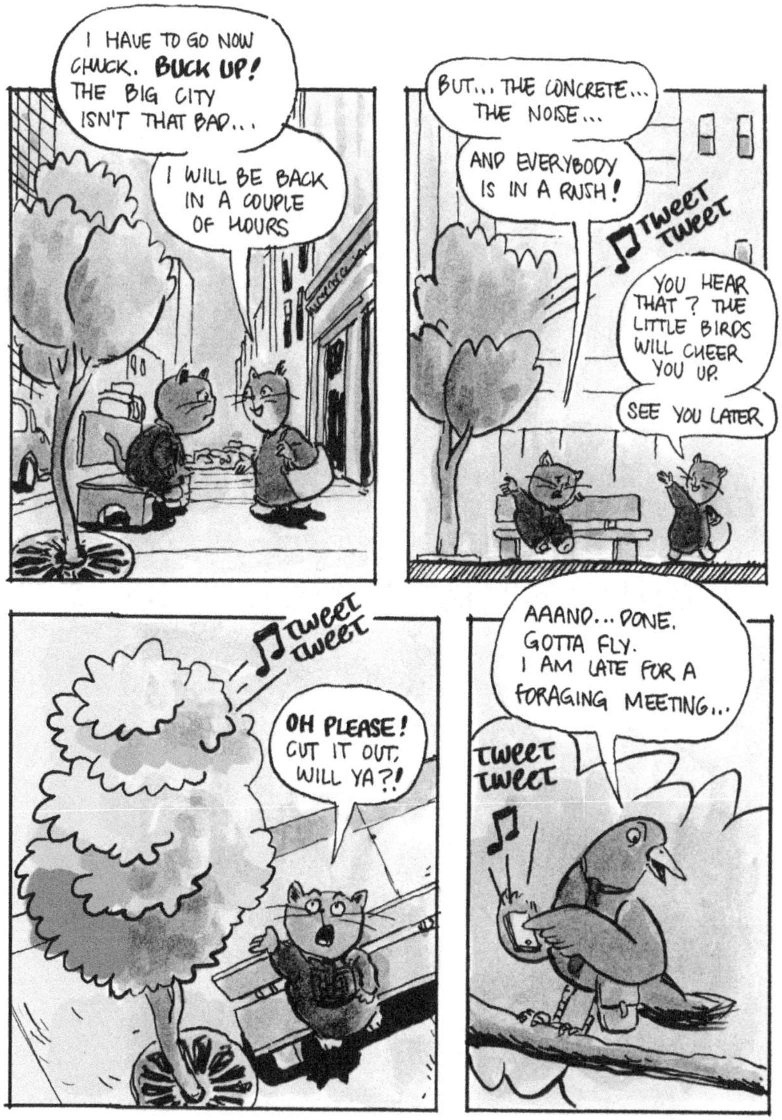

I HAVE TO GO NOW CHUCK. **BUCK UP!** THE BIG CITY ISN'T THAT BAD...
I WILL BE BACK IN A COUPLE OF HOURS
BUT... THE CONCRETE... THE NOISE...
AND EVERYBODY IS IN A RUSH!
TWEET TWEET
YOU HEAR THAT? THE LITTLE BIRDS WILL CHEER YOU UP.
SEE YOU LATER
TWEET TWEET
OH PLEASE! CUT IT OUT, WILL YA?!
AAAND... DONE. GOTTA FLY. I AM LATE FOR A FORAGING MEETING...
TWEET TWEET

Advaita: Non duality.
Same same with clapping and booing!

Question

THE NINE LIVES THEATER
TO BE IS NOT TO BE...
THERE ARE NO QUESTIONS
THERE IS ONE QUESTION
WHERE CAN WE GET OUR MONEY BACK?

This is also why you don't see any cats around during Jedi's fights!

Complicated

SO... WHEN DID YOU START FEELING THAT YOU NEEDED A BREAK FROM WORK?
WELL, THERE WAS A GRADUAL SPROUT OF INTUITION. I BECAME LESS CONCEPTUAL... MORE INSTINCTIVE. SOME THINGS GOT COMPLICATED
REALLY? LIKE WHAT? ANYTHING IN PARTICULAR?
AS THESE DATA CLEARLY INDICA... HEY!
NOT REALLY... MORE LIKE, IN GENERAL

Bullying might break some bones,
but don't forget:
It comes always from a broken heart.

Spider

WHAT ARE YOU DOING THERE, CHUCK?
I WANT TO SET FREE THE POOR FLY, BEFORE THE SPIDER EATS IT
IF YOU UNDERSTAND THE SUFFERING OF THE FLY, BUT YOU DON'T UNDERSTAND THE SUFFERING OF THE SPIDER, THEN YOU DON'T UNDERSTAND SUFFERING AT ALL
GO AHEAD! TOUCH IT "TOUGH GUY"
MAKE MY DAY

Rub them all with butter,
they will get along beautifully!

Conference

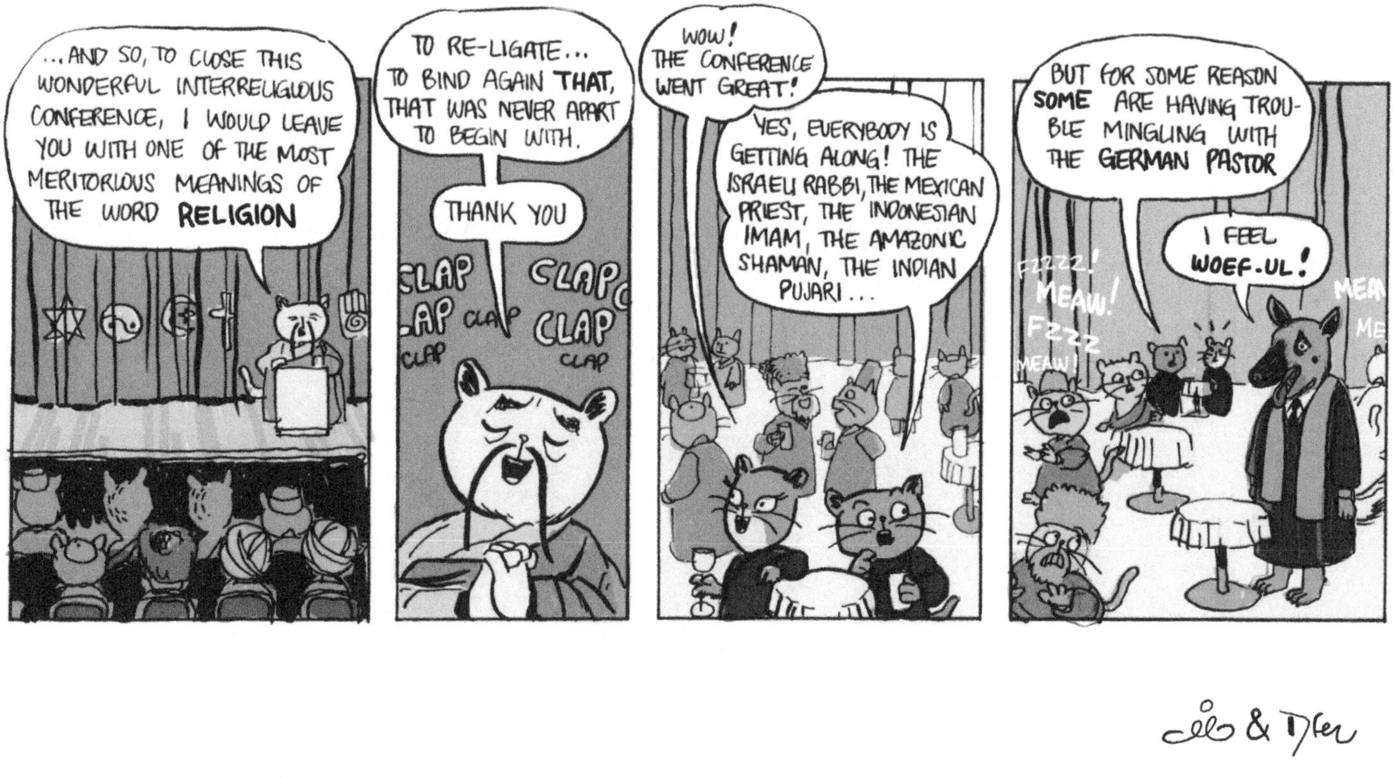

...AND SO, TO CLOSE THIS WONDERFUL INTERRELIGIOUS CONFERENCE, I WOULD LEAVE YOU WITH ONE OF THE MOST MERITORIOUS MEANINGS OF THE WORD **RELIGION**
TO RE-LIGATE... TO BIND AGAIN **THAT**, THAT WAS NEVER APART TO BEGIN WITH.
THANK YOU
CLAP CLAP CLAP CLAP CLAP CLAP CLAP
WOW! THE CONFERENCE WENT GREAT!
YES, EVERYBODY IS GETTING ALONG! THE ISRAELI RABBI, THE MEXICAN PRIEST, THE INDONESIAN IMAM, THE AMAZONIC SHAMAN, THE INDIAN PUJARI...
BUT FOR SOME REASON **SOME** ARE HAVING TROUBLE MINGLING WITH THE **GERMAN PASTOR**
I FEEL **WOEF-UL**!
FZZZZ! MEAW! FZZZ MEAW!

Release the kraken!
Gently.

Beast

ROAAAR!
THE TRICK IS BEING A POLITE BEAST.
YEAH, YOU KEEP TELLING YOURSELF THAT!

Success is a measure
decided by others.
Satisfaction is a measure
decided by you.

— Unknown

Reward

AND HERE, WE INVESTIGATE THE EXTENT TO WHICH SUBJECTS ARE WILLING TO MAKE AN EXTREME EFFORT FOR A MINIMUM REWARD
WOW!
YEAH! THEY PRESS A LEVER TO GET FOOD AND CAN DEVOTE ENORMOUS AMOUNTS OF BEHAVIOR IN EXCHANGE FOR ALMOST NOTHING
OK BUDDY, GOTTA GO. I HAVE A TON OF STUFF TO DO. SEE YOU LATER. YOU KNOW YOUR WAY AROUND
OH...OK. NO WORRIES. SEE YOU LATER
?
WHAT THE HECK ARE YOU DOING HERE?
I AM MAKING A CAREER IN SCIENCE
AND YOU WILL **NEVER** STOP ME!

Warning:
Objects in the mind are
smaller than they appear.

Obstacle

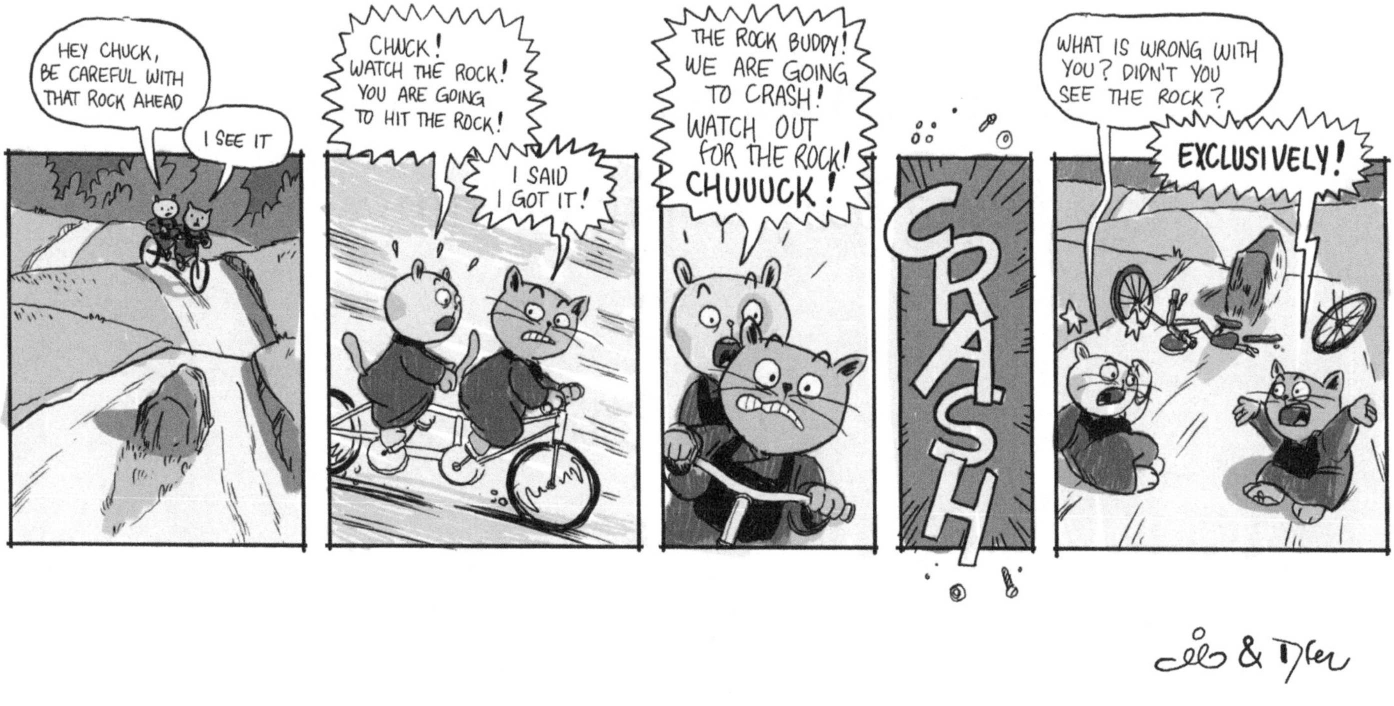

HEY CHUCK, BE CAREFUL WITH THAT ROCK AHEAD
I SEE IT
CHUCK! WATCH THE ROCK! YOU ARE GOING TO HIT THE ROCK!
I SAID I GOT IT!
THE ROCK BUDDY! WE ARE GOING TO CRASH! WATCH OUT FOR THE ROCK! CHUUUCK!
CRASH
WHAT IS WRONG WITH YOU? DIDN'T YOU SEE THE ROCK?
EXCLUSIVELY!

Doing nothing is better than being busy doing nothing.

— Lao Tzu

Start

DIIING
SENSEI, HOW DID YOU START PRACTICING ZAZEN?
OH, I LISTENED TO THE WORDS OF A VERY WISE WOMAN
REALLY?
WHO?
MY EX-WIFE
SHE ALWAYS INSISTED ON HOW GOOD I WAS AT SITTING ON MY BUTT, DOING NOTHING!

Check the stick holding that dangling carrot.
You might want to see what it is attached to.

Chase

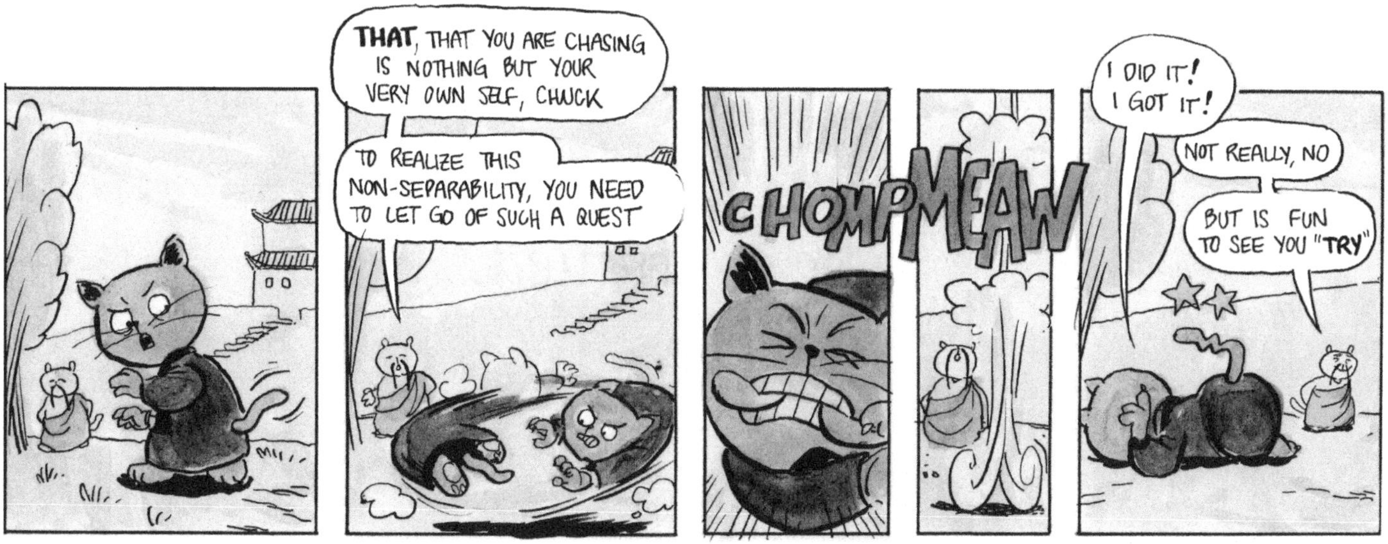
THAT, THAT YOU ARE CHASING IS NOTHING BUT YOUR VERY OWN SELF, CHUCK
TO REALIZE THIS NON-SEPARABILITY, YOU NEED TO LET GO OF SUCH A QUEST
CHOMP MEAW
I DID IT! I GOT IT!
NOT REALLY, NO
BUT IS FUN TO SEE YOU "TRY"

To be continued...

Acknowledgments

Carlos would like to express his deepest gratitude to The Practice, The Way. Also his very special thanks to Patricia, Nelly, Guillermo and Catalina for their invaluable support in his life and during the development of this project. To Diego for walking along, to the lovely readers and to all his friends and family who are an inexhaustible source of motivation, learning, compassion, and inspiration.

Diego would like to thank his wife Carolina for making sooo much time for him to sit down and work on the strips over weekends, and for her enthusiasm and support. Also to his kids, Nico and Sebas, whom he enjoyed so much watching them draw little Chucks with various techniques. Lastly, to Carlos, for his patience and perseverance.

Both authors would like to thank the editorial comments and suggestions of Christian Teubner, Phil Brudie, Ryan McAllister and Patricia Cerdá. Finally, they want to express their profound gratitude to the Kickstarter's backers that made the first printed version of this book possible.

Gassho

Chuck online

Please share your mind with us, we are very interested in listening. Drop us a couple of lines in our contact section.

Our strips are available online in English, Spanish and Dutch. Make sure you check our books section every once in a while in case you want some language alternatives.

Also, if you are interested in supporting our project, you can make a Fuse (Dana) in our online begging bowl to keep this kitty purring.

Best purrs,

Chuck the monk

www.chuckthemonk.com

Thank you for supporting an honest and heartful initiative.

3% of our earnings are donated to the NGO School for Life
(Colombia - Germany)
www.escuelaparalavida.org
www.schulefuersleben.de

The making-of...

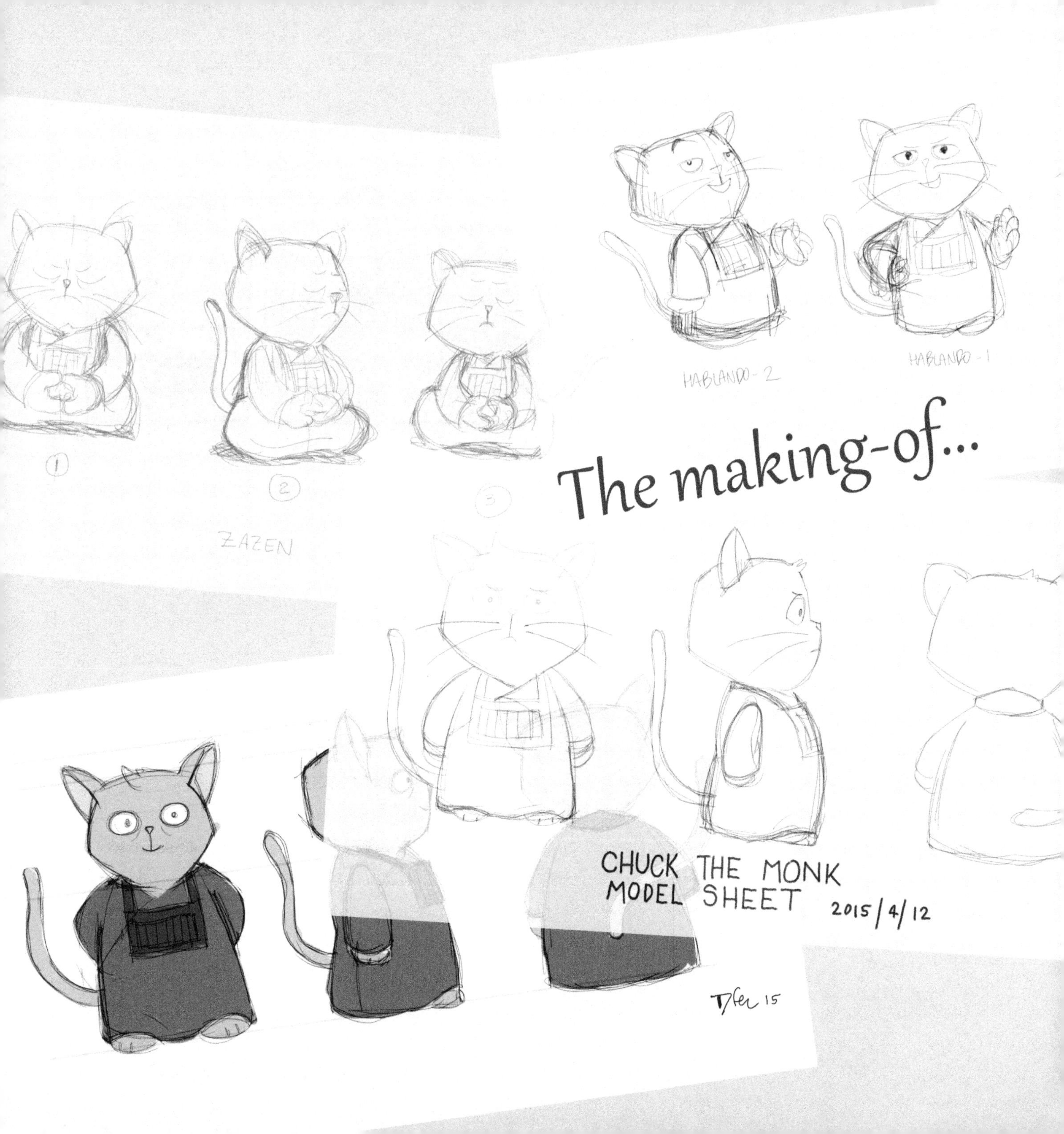

1
2
3
ZAZEN
HABLANDO-2
HABLANDO-1
CHUCK THE MONK
MODEL SHEET
2015/4/12

Finding the right proportions for drawing me is not an easy task, although I am hoping it is an enjoyable one. Carlos and Diego go back and forth searching for the right drawings that fit my personality or my actions, like the one on the left where I am practicing Zazen.

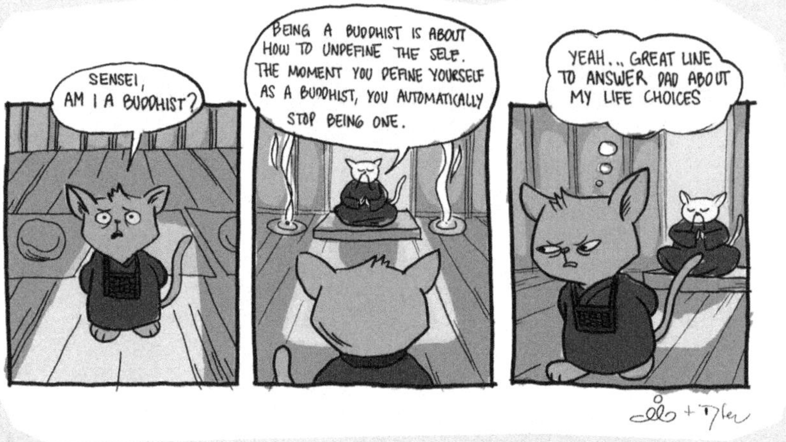

SENSEI, AM I A BUDDHIST?
BEING A BUDDHIST IS ABOUT HOW TO UNDEFINE THE SELF. THE MOMENT YOU DEFINE YOURSELF AS A BUDDHIST, YOU AUTOMATICALLY STOP BEING ONE.
YEAH... GREAT LINE TO ANSWER DAD ABOUT MY LIFE CHOICES

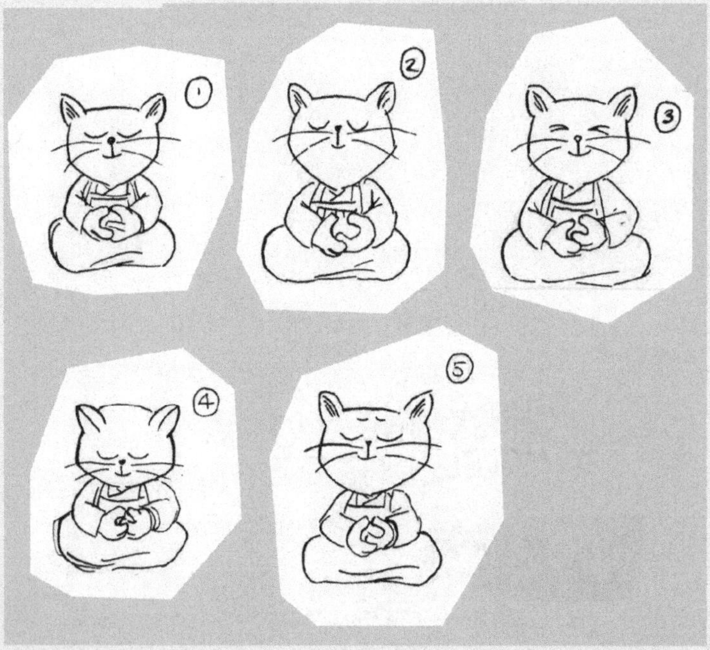

1
2
3
4
5

Even for the zafus, they explore different shapes so that they would have the character needed for the strip. I mean, c'mon, how hard can it be to draw a cushion?

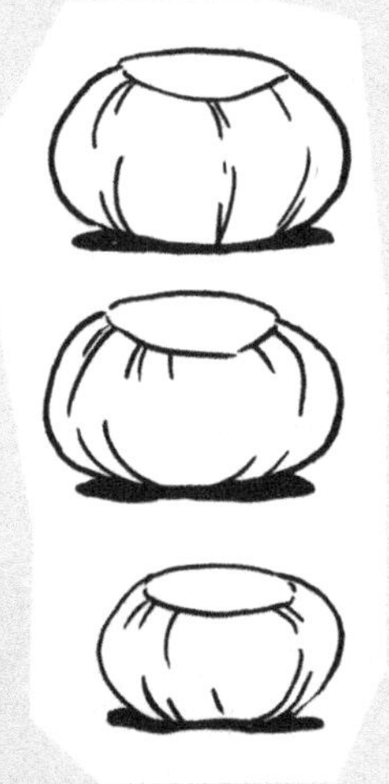

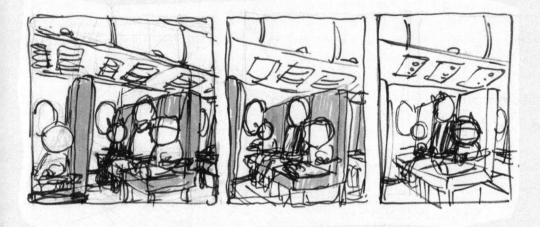

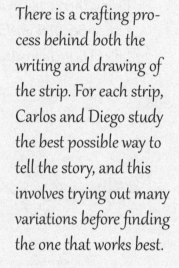

There is a crafting process behind both the writing and drawing of the strip. For each strip, Carlos and Diego study the best possible way to tell the story, and this involves trying out many variations before finding the one that works best.

Below, there's me in a hammock. I remember that one! but apparently, it takes Diego many tries to get it right!

Sometimes the "extras" like the German Shepherd on one of the strips also require some studying.

On the right, there is a great shot of me chasing my tail.

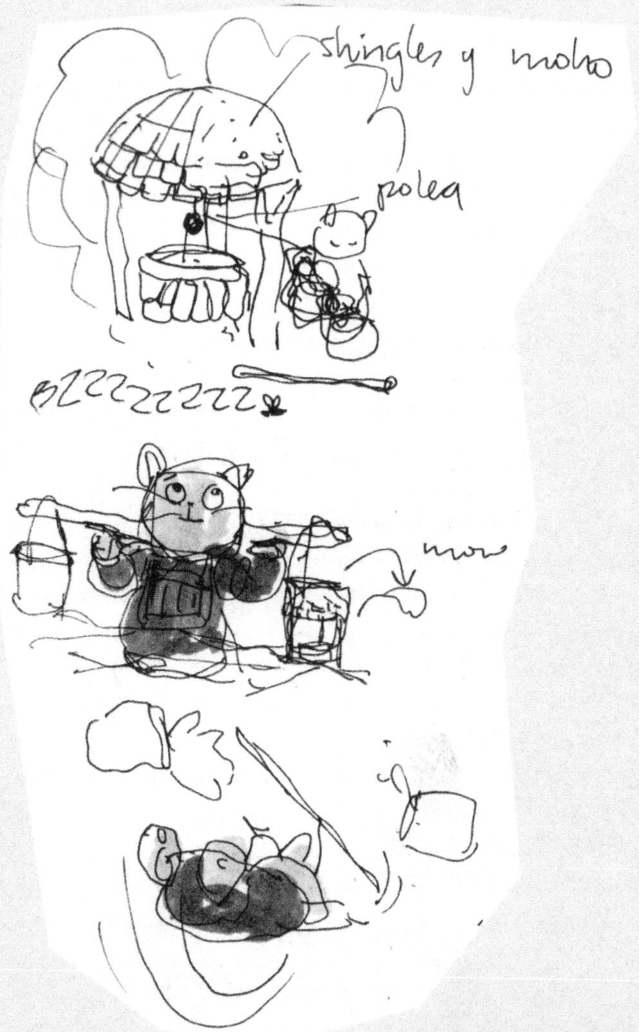
shingles y moho
polea

For some strips, the location is very important, for others, the interaction between characters becomes fundamental, like the strip below, where I am having a conversation with my dear grandma. You will get to see that story in our next book!

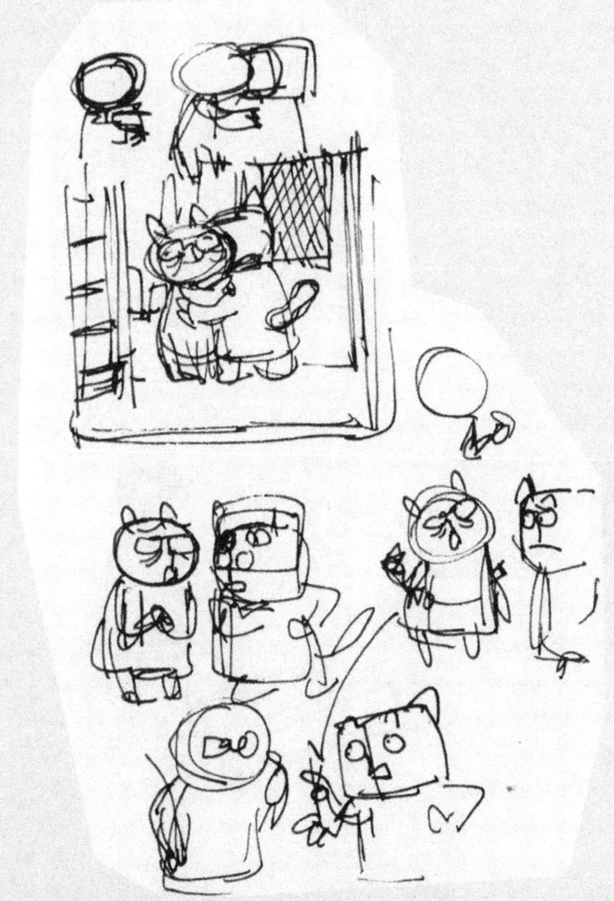

Psycho Tobi with a knife.
Not a good combination.

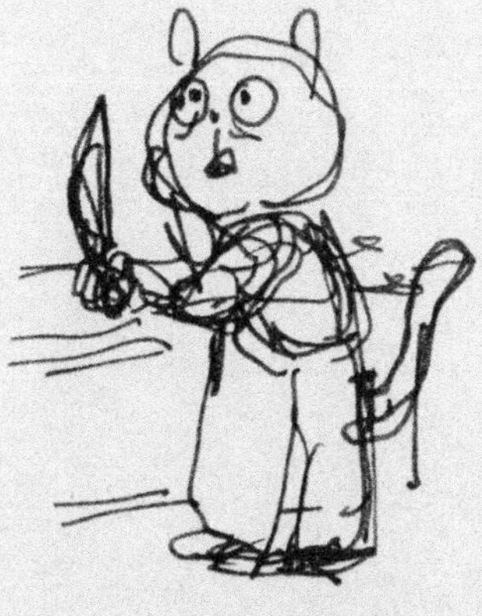

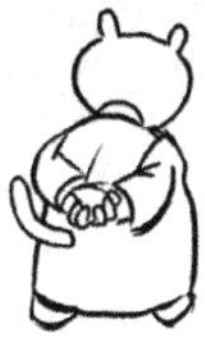

About the authors

The happening of me was the product of cosmic convergence. Diego and Carlos went to school together and were good friends as kids. Adolescence drove them apart and adulthood brought them together again. While living abroad, these two friends visited their families and met again after many years.

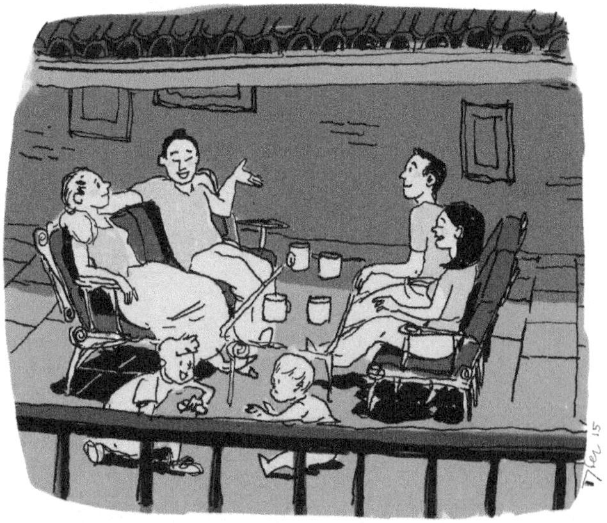

Over dinner, their mutual confessions about meditation became a spark in the dark: Carlos smoothed out some wrinkly notes and Diego unsheathed a pencil. That is how I was born.

After many years in NYC and Portland, Diego is currently back home with his family. He is glad that architecture, wife, kids, mortgage, and drawing keep him very busy and still manages to be a serious meditation practitioner. Carlos, trying to find (or running away from) something, travels constantly since he was a kid. He is both a brain scientist and an ordained monk within the Zen tradition.

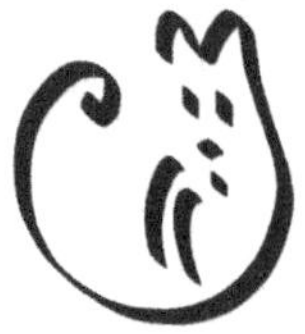

Chuck the monk